Cases, Causes and Controversies

Fifty Tales from the Law

by James Wilson

Wildy, Simmonds & Hill Publishing

First published in Great Britain 2012 by Wildy, Simmonds & Hill Publishing

Website: www.wildy.com

Wilson, James

Cases, Causes and Controversies: Fifty Tales from the Law

ISBN 9780854901258

Printed and bound in Great Britain

To Sam and Aran

Contents

Acknowledgements

In Alan Bridges' 1985 film *The Shooting Party*, James Mason's character Sir Randolph Nettleby says to a grandchild "It is always good to spend part of each day writing down your thoughts. That way you will not have to bother others with them." In my case I have breached that sound aphorism: having written a number of thoughts down, I then had the temerity to bother many people with them. They in turn were kind enough to offer a large number of comments, questions and suggestions on the articles which have now become this book.

First and foremost were the excellent editorial teams in charge of Magazines and Journals at LexisNexis, where most of the pieces were first published: Elsa Booth, Jan Miller, Diana Rose, Rebecca Smith, Charles Kloet, Danielle Munroe, Sarah Plaka and Christina Gregoriou. Next were the two friends who co-authored pieces with me: Lynne Townley of the Crown Prosecution Service and Anne-Marie Forker of LexisNexis.

Then there was a substantial cast of unpaid proofreaders, otherwise known as friends, family and colleagues. Their numbers included Sally Barker, Simon Clarke, Vanessa Cortis, Toby Frost, Helen Redding, Craig Rose, Helen Sheridan, Guy Skelton, Lisa Townsend, and my parents Bob and Penny Wilson. Needless to say, all remaining errors are my own.

I also owe a debt to Helens Redding and Sheridan for advice on publishing.

Finally, and most importantly, thanks to my wife Mona and our two children Sam and Aran for their love and support throughout.

No doubt there are several others I have accidentally omitted – perhaps many – to whom I offer belated thanks and apologies.

Acknowledgements

Introduction

The well-known American legal scholar Robert S. Summers once wrote:

> "The published justifications appearing in opinions of the higher courts in Western legal systems comprise what is perhaps the greatest repository of recorded practical reasoning known to humankind."
>
> Neil MacCormick and Robert S Summers (eds), *Interpreting Statutes: A Comparative Study* (1991) p 1.

It is a bold claim, but Professor Summers could cite an almost continuous process from the first year book in 1291 to the more familiar law reports of the present day, and it is hard to think of a comparable intellectual compendium that might mount a serious challenge.

Legal reasoning, being a unique mixture of philosophy, ethics, logic, semantic interpretation, grammatical pedantry, guesswork, invention and literature, is interesting enough in itself. But it is only half of what is in the law reports. The other half is the human story of who has come to court and why. In this respect the best cases constitute the high – or low – points of human dramas so improbable or absurd they would simply not be credible if they did not happen to be true.

This book is about cases that reflect those two aspects of the interest and allure of case law. It is intended to be an interesting read with a distinctly lighter touch than one would find in academic journals, but also with serious points throughout.

It is essentially a compilation of articles I have written over the past two years for several different publications, primarily *New Law Journal, Criminal Law & Justice Weekly,* and *Halsbury's Law Exchange* and my own blog *A(nother) lawyer writes* (www.timesandotherthings.blogspot.com). Some I have edited slightly, usually to add a few points which the original word limits precluded. Here and there I have added an afterword to expand on the arguments or to bring the story up to date.

Although there was no grand scheme, the articles reflected my own interests and therefore rather naturally fell into a series of patterns – criminal law, military history, human rights, free speech and so on. The book is divided into separate parts accordingly, and I have written a short introduction for each.

Many of the articles were prompted by cases and other legal stories making the headlines at the time, particularly those concerning human rights. In this respect a number of repetitive questions arose in different cases – how to balance freedom of religion, freedom of speech and the right to gender and sexual equality.

Of course most such issues are not new, but since the Human Rights Act 1998 came into force they have to be determined within the framework of the European Convention on Human Rights. There is never likely to be a consensus on their resolution, and therefore I suspect they now form a permanent feature of the British political landscape.

At all times I tried to avoid technical legal words and phrases, and to ensure no background legal knowledge was necessary.

Naturally I would not expect everyone to agree with all of my arguments, but if they stimulate some thought and debate then I will have achieved more than I set out to do. For the most part the articles in this book were written simply because I enjoyed doing so. I hope that is reflected in how they read.

Part I: Victorian Murders

The genre of "Victorian Murders" has long had a hold on the public imagination, be it in fiction with the likes of Sherlock Holmes, or in real life with killers such as Jack the Ripper. Respectively those two constitute the most famous fictional detective and the most famous real-life criminal in English history. Indeed, George Orwell thought the Victorian period formed part of the "finest age of murders":

> "If one examines the murders which have given the greatest amount of pleasure to the British public, the murders whose story is known in its general outline to almost everyone and which have been made into novels and re-hashed over and over again by the Sunday papers, one finds a fairly strong family resemblance running through the greater number of them. Our great period in murder, our Elizabethan period, so to speak, seems to have been between roughly 1850 and 1925. "

("Decline of the English Murder", *Tribune*, 15 February 1946.)

Two of the cases I have chosen are amongst the best known in the common law. The first is that of Daniel M'Naghten. It established the legal definition of insanity, which has stood for more than a century and a half. I have avoided writing about the implications of the legal holding in M'Naghten's case, though what constitutes insanity is a complex and important issue. This is primarily because there has already been so much written on the topic, but also because the underlying conspiracy in the actual case is an intriguing story unto itself, although much less well known.

The other classic common law case is *R v Dudley and Stephens,* where the opposite applies – the facts are very well known, but the actual legal principle was not dealt with impressively in the case itself and therefore lends itself to further consideration.

Sandwiched between those two is the tale of John "Babbacombe" Lee, better known as "the man they couldn't hang". Lee entered popular culture by the great drama of a failed execution, and, as with M'Naghten, the popularity of his case is heightened by mystery. In Lee's case the mystery is twofold: why the hanging failed, and whether he had been guilty in the first place. As with all good mysteries the truth can never be known. As it happens, the memoirs of his would-have-been hangman, James Berry, can be found free online and formed one of the most interesting of all the books I read as part of the research for this book.

1. A Victorian murder-mystery

To date the only British Prime Minister to have been assassinated is the unfortunate Sir Spencer Perceval (1762-1812), and his place as a regular answer in pub quizzes across the land is thereby assured. No doubt there have been many other attempts, and indeed the total number of failed attempts can never be known.

One alleged attempt forms the background to one of the most famous cases in English legal history, that of Daniel M'Naghten, whose case has framed the legal test for insanity for over a century and a half. Every lawyer will have heard of the case for that reason.

Not so many, however, would know that the factual background to the case involves a rather intriguing conspiracy theory.

For most of his life, in the early to mid-nineteenth century, M'Naghten lived largely anonymously as a wood-turner, although he had a few other interests as well. Among other things, he tried his hand at acting for three years, taught himself French, attended a debating society, travelled to France and attended anatomy classes at Glasgow University – all of which amounted to fairly advanced pastimes for a Victorian artisan, one would have thought ... But inevitably much of the detail of his life is rather sketchy.

What we do know is that somewhere amongst those seemingly random activities he formed the view that the Tories had it in for him. He reported this concern to the police and alleged that he was being tracked by "Tory spies".

No one believed a word of it or otherwise paid him much attention at the time, but in January 1843 he took a step towards legal immortality when he shot and killed a civil servant, Edward Drummond. He made his one and

Published in the *New Law Journal*, vol 160, 3 December 2010, p 1688 only public statement on the affair in the magistrates' court the following day, in which he lumped the blame on the Tories for having "entirely destroyed my peace of mind" (a complaint which, fortunately, does not usually suffice to apportion blame for murder).

An improbably large sum of money for the day (£750) was found on him, and this was used to fund a formidable legal defence team, assembled with great speed. At trial the issue was the definition of legal insanity, and the ensuing holding still represents the single most important statement of that definition in English law.

M'Naghten's name is accordingly still cited in the law reports more than a century and a half later. Yet it has left unresolved the question of the true purpose of his shooting Drummond that day. Why did he have such a large amount of money on him? Where did he get it from, given the generally modestly lucrative nature of his legitimate occupation?

Most assume that M'Naghten had not intended to kill Drummond at all, but rather the Prime Minister of the day, Sir Robert Peel, and that the money was paid to him to carry out the hit. Perhaps, therefore, the conspiracy runs, M'Naghten wasn't mad at all, but made up the vague ramblings about delusions in the hope of escaping the gallows (if so, it wasn't much mitigation, as he spent the rest of his life in a lunatic asylum).

As conspiracy theories go it seems plausible enough, at least on the basis that Drummond was hardly an obvious target for a political assassination. He had been a civil servant most of his life, and at the time was personal secretary to Peel. It was while en route from Peel's house to Downing Street that he was shot by M'Naghten, so it is easy enough to believe M'Naghten thought he was killing Peel himself. After all, it was not the age of television and Peel's appearance would therefore have been far less well known than that of any modern holder of the office.

Such is the conclusion of no less an authority than the Dictionary of National Biography. Even if one believes M'Naghten aimed at the wrong man, however, we are still left with some difficult and intriguing questions. First, who paid him the money? Someone or some people very wealthy, one assumes.

Secondly, what persuaded such wealthy benefactors to assume that M'Naghten was a suitable assassin? Did he have a proven record in the field that has been lost with time? If not, and indeed if he truly was insane, then he wasn't much of a choice.

Thirdly, was the £750 paid in full and final settlement of M'Naghten's services to be rendered? If so, then the backer(s) had to have been pretty confident that he was going to do as he agreed rather than scarper – and indeed that he would succeed in doing it.

Well, who knows. It is hardly the only famous Victorian murder mystery to remain unsolved, and indeed insoluble.

2. Escaping the noose

Everyone makes mistakes. But not all mistakes have equal consequences. Bankers' mistakes might cost billions. Pilots' mistakes might cost lives, as might those of surgeons. By contrast, in the now-defunct vocation of hangman, mistakes by the practitioner actually saved lives. Several episodes of the classic 1950s television series *The Twilight Zone* featured stories of people escaping the noose, usually to receive their just desserts in a more macabre fashion. But, as ever, real life supplies the most bizarre examples.

On Christmas Eve 1705, for example, one John Smith survived swinging from the gallows pole for 15 minutes before the growing agitation of the assembled crowd led to him being reprieved. Some years later, in 1740, William Duell was hanged and his body taken to Surgeons' Hall to be put to use in medical science. As he was placed on the table, it was noticed that he was still breathing, and shortly afterwards he was able to sit up in his chair and went on to make a full recovery.

In 1803, Joseph Samuel, one of Australia's earliest Jewish settlers (via the convict route, having committed a robbery in England), was scheduled to be hanged for murder in New South Wales. A large crowd assembled, only to watch the rope break on the first attempt, slip on the second, and break again on the third. After that the State Governor took the view that it was a "sign from God" that Samuel should not be executed, although he did not take it as a sign that Samuel was innocent, and so commuted the sentence to life imprisonment instead.

Perhaps the most famous example is that of John Henry George Lee, better known to history as John "Babbacombe" Lee. Born in 1864, Lee served in the Navy before being invalided out. He found employment as a footman in the residence of one Emma Keyse in a house in Babbacombe, Devon, known as "The Glen". In 1884 Miss Keyse was found murdered: her throat had been cut, she had head wounds and the killer had apparently tried to burn the body and start fires elsewhere in the house. Lee had been the only male in the house at the time, and had a cut on his forearm, but the evidence did not go much further than that. He had a previous conviction for theft from his employer, which doubtless led some to infer a motive. Despite maintaining his innocence, he was convicted of murder and sentenced to death.

The date of the hanging was set for 23 February 1885. The hangman was the relatively inexperienced James Berry, who had only been appointed to his role the previous year. He inspected the trapdoor and confirmed it was in working order, but when Lee stood upon it nothing happened. The procedure was repeated twice more: each time Berry confirmed the trapdoor was working properly but each time it failed to open when Lee stood upon it.

The hanging was postponed and then cancelled as Lee's sentence was commuted to life imprisonment by Sir William Harcourt, the Home Secretary. Harcourt took the view that "[i]t would shock the feeling of anyone if a man had twice to pay the pangs of imminent death."

Berry himself later blamed the quality of the iron catches and the woodwork of the doors. Other suggestions included the wood having been swollen by recent rain, or even Berry being paid off by Lee or his supporters.

Lee was eventually released after serving 22 years, still maintaining his innocence. Not surprisingly records are not entirely clear as to the rest of his days, but there seems to be some evidence that he lived until 1945. Some sources claim he died in the United States, whilst others maintain his final years were in London. If the latter, he would have lived through the Blitz, where, contrary to Harcourt's feelings, he would have to have had to endure the pangs of imminent death on many more occasions ...

The life of the hangman Berry is rather better documented. He was the first hangman to be literate enough to publish his own memoirs, in which he described Lee as having been "perfectly calm, almost indifferent" on arrival and remained like a statue throughout the failed execution.

Despite his hapless start with Lee, and another mistake in which he was thought to have gone too far in the other direction by almost decapitating the prisoner, Berry went on to make various refinements to the process which remained standard practice until the abolition of capital punishment in the mid-twentieth century. In all, he undertook 131 hangings in a seven-year career.

Nevertheless Berry has been largely forgotten since. It was Lee who became known in popular culture, referenced in songs, a silent film and a play as well as the inevitable ghost stories and local myths. From time to time the media have reinvestigated the case, usually either concluding that the evidence remains insufficient or advancing some new and rather florid conspiracy as to the murderer's true identity. One recent example is the BBC's Inside Out programme, which in 2007 suggested that Lee's own solicitor, Reginald Templar, might have been a worthy suspect. Templar had been a frequent visitor to The Glen and seemed to offer his services to Lee rather too promptly after the murder.

The programme conceded, however, that the evidence was no better against either man, and so the case will remain another unsolved Victorian murder mystery for future Orwells to pore over.

3. Necessity as a defence to murder

Two media stories in 2010 of great human interest but with tragically different outcomes were those of the trapped miners in Chile and in New Zealand. No insensitivity to the families of the New Zealand mining disaster victims is intended hereby, but the possibility of men trapped in such a manner raises one of the classic problems of criminal law and jurisprudence – namely, how far the rules of civilised society can apply in wholly exceptional circumstances.

Suppose a group of people were trapped and could not be reached in time to prevent starvation without them resorting to cannibalism. That was the scenario envisaged by Lon Fuller in his classic essay "The Case of the Speluncean Explorers" (*Harvard Law Review*, vol 62, no 4, p 616). Fuller's inspiration was one of the most infamous cases in English law, *R v Dudley and Stephens* [1881-85] All ER Rep 61, the case of the shipwrecked sailors killing and eating the luckless cabin boy.

The facts are well known. The case concerned the vessel *Mignonette*, a 16 m cruiser built in 1867. She was purchased in 1883 by an Australian lawyer, John Henry Want, who hired a crew of four to sail her to Sydney: Tom Dudley, Edwin Stephens, Edmund Brooks and Richard Parker. Dudley was captain and Parker, aged 17, filled the role of cabin boy.

During the voyage a wave struck the vessel and the crew escaped into a lifeboat, with only two tins of turnips and no fresh water. They managed to capture a turtle which drew out the food a bit longer, but soon reached the stage of drinking their own urine, along with some seawater which only made things worse.

Shorter version published in *Criminal Law & Justice Weekly*, vol 175, 7 May 2011, p 270

A few days later they became so desperate that cannibalism seemed the only option. Brooks refused to entertain the possibility, but the other two went ahead with the deed of killing Parker (who was probably comatose by that stage), following which all three fed upon his body.

Famously the three survivors were rescued shortly afterwards, and the two who had carried out the killing found themselves on trial for murder. They were convicted after Lord Chief Justice Coleridge ruled that necessity is no defence to murder.

In a modern review of the case ("Death on the High Seas" in *Cases that Changed Our Lives*, LexisNexis 2010), David Perry QC laments the modest standard of the legal reasoning in the case, which makes it surprising that it still remains authority for Coleridge LCJ's principle. It is therefore worth questioning whether the principle is justifiable.

Mr Perry QC recounts the following hypothetical problem, like the case itself, a ubiquitous feature of law and moral philosophy tutorials. Suppose you are in charge of a set of railway points. A train is coming down the line which is going to hit five people. There is no time to stop the train or warn the people. The only option is to switch the points and send the train onto another line, where there is only one person. Should you intervene and cause the death of the one in order to save the five? Suppose the one is a woman and the five are all men. Does one invoke the "Birkenhead rule" (women and children first) and refuse to intervene? What if the one is a child and the five all adults?

Or suppose you are a surgeon with five patients, each of whom requires a different organ transplant. No organs will be available in time. But there is another patient who requires minor surgery of a different sort. Do you take each of the necessary organs out of the one patient and thereby save the five?

Straw polls I have conducted always favour flicking the switch of the railway points, but never intervening as a surgeon. And yet it is hard to see a moral distinction.

Both are distinct from the trapped miner/shipwrecked sailor dilemma, however, in that the trapped people all face death, rather than being in control of the lives of others. How do they decide who lives? Perhaps those with the lowest chance of survival should be sacrificed, but it would be perilous for the law to place a greater value on one life than another. About the fairest solution would seem be to draw lots.

It would be rare indeed for facts to be as cut and dried as in a tutorial (how could one ever prove the draw was conducted fairly?), although the law regularly has to deal with cases with no independent evidence, and the difficulty applies equally whether the defence of necessity is available or not.

Should, therefore, the law regarding necessity be abolished, thus enabling one innocent person to kill another innocent person, if the alternative is both of them dying?

With some diffidence, I suggest that it should not. The present law might be imperfect, but there are still four safeguards against injustice. The first is the Attorney General's discretion not to bring prosecutions even where there is strong prima facie evidence of an offence having been committed. That is a fundamental principle of the criminal law.

The second is the admittedly rough sort of protection in the form of the jury system. Someone attracting overwhelming public sympathy might expect that to be reflected in the jury's decision.

The third is the flexibility in sentencing, though that is substantially reduced when the charge is one of murder.

The fourth is the very rarely used Royal Prerogative of Mercy.

It is true that in the case of a person considered morally innocent, all but the first method might leave a lingering sense of injustice, but on the other hand, for obvious reasons, extending the categories of acceptable murder – which is what a defence of necessity amounts to – has to be a step taken with the utmost reluctance. Ultimately, the injustice of a wrongful conviction can be at least partially redeemed, but the injustice of wrongfully permitting murder cannot.

Back to Dudley and Stephens themselves. Following their conviction they faced the death penalty, but the public outcry was such that the sentence was commuted to six months' imprisonment. Stephens lived until 1914 when he died in poverty. Dudley sailed to Australia once more, fairly soon after being released. One might have thought his previous experience would have put him off the sea for good, although there was probably little alternative in the harsher world of Victorian England. This time he made it without incident, but a few years later contracted and died of the plague.

Que sera sera, I suppose, or, to adopt a more pithy phrase from the vernacular, sod's law.

Part II: Hollywood on Trial

This part of the book concerns three very different cinematic legends involved in three very different cases. The first two consider one of the great stars of silent cinema and one of the first stars of "talkies", from a time in Hollywood history that was beautifully depicted in the recent Oscar-winning film *The Artist*.

Nowadays largely forgotten, Fatty Arbuckle was one of the most famous actors of his day. As we will see, he became the unhappy victim of trial by media following a ridiculous scandal. In that respect he started a trend that has never finished, as shown by the recent contempt of court case arising out of the murder of Joanna Yeates, which is discussed later in this book.

Bette Davis's star was on the rise around the time of Arbuckle's premature death. Her case did not involve anything salacious like Arbuckle's or tawdry like that of the third case in this part, Roman Polanski. But it is a window into the very different world of Hollywood in the 1930s, when the relationship between stars and studios was weighted heavily in the latter's favour and gender equality was a largely unknown concept in employment law (or anywhere else). Indeed the very term "gender equality" would have first befuddled and then affronted most people of the time.

It is true that a select few women had been making serious money since the silent era. Lillian Gish, for example, had paved the way in several DW Griffiths epics, while those with a grasp of Latin might appreciate a joke of the time that ran *Sic Transit Gloria Swanson*. It is nevertheless indisputable that opportunities for independent women were much fewer then than now.

With that in mind it was mildly disingenuous for Warner Bros' counsel to have assured the court that Davis had the wit and ability not to need the income from films if she did not to want to make any – wit and ability she certainly had, but it is not clear how she might have employed those attributes in an equally lucrative fashion in those days outside of stage or screen.

Even in the slightly unreal world of cinema there can be very few individuals who have led such an extraordinary life as Roman Polanski. There are also very few films I admire more than *The Pianist* or *Chinatown*. It is true that none of Mr Polanski's personal tragedies or artistic triumphs can excuse the crime for which he pleaded guilty in 1977. Then again, neither can – or should – a single crime extinguish his human rights. For that reason I have concluded, not without considerable hesitation, that it was right that he was allowed to give evidence in his civil claim for libel by videolink to avoid any risk of extradition for his unrelated crimes. Having said that, I have not commented about whether he should have been able to bring an action for libel at all – it does seem to me that English libel laws are weighted too heavily in favour of the claimant, to the detriment of free speech.

4. Template for the pitfalls of fame: the Fatty Arbuckle story

One common playground insult when I was at primary school was "Fatty Arbuckle". I doubt any of us knew the origin of the name, any more than we later did as patrons of the American-style restaurant chain. A little over 60 years earlier, however, Roscoe "Fatty" Arbuckle (he despised the nickname) had undergone three criminal trials as famous – or infamous – in their day as any that have followed. As a case which involved a famous person, wild press speculation and a politically motivated prosecutor, and yet whose fame vanished in short order, it was one of Hollywood's most striking early portents.

The nickname Arbuckle detested derived from his size – he weighed about 300 pounds as an adult – yet he remained strikingly agile, as any of his silent films (extracts of which are easily found on the internet) attest.

At the start of his career acting was not a reputable profession: the local equivalent to B&Bs were known to have signs proclaiming "no dogs or actors allowed". If anything, screen actors were seen as an even lower form than their stage brethren. Arbuckle nevertheless aimed in that direction by joining the famous Keystone studios, and regularly appeared as one of the eponymous cops. He became the master of the staple silent comedy device of throwing pies (and, given the maintenance of his physique, presumably eating them as well). He mentored both Buster Keaton and Charlie Chaplin and for that reason alone deserves cinematic immortality.

In 1918 Arbuckle made history by being awarded the first million dollar film contract. Of course there was a Faustian element – the studio demanded a formidable schedule of film-making in return. In September 1921, exhausted by the workload, Arbuckle went on a short

Published in the *New Law Journal*, vol 161, 12 August 2011, p 1150.

holiday. With two friends he checked into a hotel in San Francisco. They invited a few guests for a party, two of whom would prove to be about the least suitable attendees imaginable.

One was Virginia Rappé, a 26 year old would-be actress. Another was one Bambina Maude Delmont, who had had a number of criminal convictions, most relevantly for fraud and extortion.

The undisputed facts were that Rappé collapsed during the evening and was discovered by Arbuckle. The disputed facts were very many.

Rappé was seen by the hotel doctor but not admitted to hospital until two days later; within a further 24 hours she died of peritonitis caused by a ruptured bladder.

Although no suggestion of rape had been made by any of the doctors who examined her before death, and her medical history suggested an obvious cause for abdominal problems (she had had several abortions – a risky procedure at the time which was often undertaken by less than reputable surgeons), an accusation was nevertheless made by Delmont, and Arbuckle found himself charged with rape and manslaughter.

At this point the pitfalls of fame coupled with the ubiquitous human fault of greed came into play. Rappé's manager publicly accused Arbuckle of having committed rape with a piece of ice. The tabloid press picked up the story and ran with it. Chief villain amongst them was William Randolph Hearst, who controlled a national newspaper chain and knew a saleable story when he saw one. Lurid story after lurid story appeared, suggesting rape with various implements, and any other accusations the press considered outré. (Hollywood would later have its revenge of sorts on Hearst, with the film à clef of Citizen Kane clearly directed at him, much to his fury …)

Medical evidence gave no suggestion of external force against Rappé. Nor was there any direct witness to any assault by Arbuckle (least of all Delmont, who wasn't called by the prosecution, who had realised how easily she would have been discredited). But the jury could not agree, being split 10-2 (in Arbuckle's favour), and so a retrial was ordered.

The second trial ended with a second hung jury, this time 9-3 favouring conviction, following what seems to have been a more lacklustre defence, Arbuckle not taking the stand for example.

In the third trial the jury had no doubt, returning a not-guilty verdict within minutes. Most of their deliberations were spent composing a note expressing in ringing tones their belief in Arbuckle's innocence and their great regret for what he had been through.

That should have been that, but of course things were not so simple. Arbuckle had been devastated financially and now found himself virtually unemployable. Then as now, strong moralistic pressure groups were active in American politics, and they saw their chance to clamp down on Hollywood. Their efforts led to the introduction of "morality clauses" in actors' contracts.

Arbuckle managed a few jobbing directing roles for the rest of the decade, but redemption finally followed in 1933 when he signed with Warner Bros to make a feature film. With some considerable pathos he died the same day.

Ninety years later the weight of modern opinion is overwhelmingly in favour of his innocence. The case might have been the first true Hollywood scandal but it was, needless to say, very far from the last.

The subsequent saga that perhaps comes closest to Arbuckle's for mistrial by media is the OJ Simpson trial of the mid-1990s. One wonders if his case will vanish from general public knowledge within the same sort of time frame as Arbuckle's. If it does, we can be sure a replacement will soon follow.

5. A screen siren comes to court

In 1931 a young American actress achieved every aspiring thespian's dream: a contract with a major Hollywood studio. She was not particularly well known at the time, but soon gained critical and commercial acclaim, enabling her to renegotiate her contract on more favourable terms a few years later.

Nevertheless, she became disillusioned with the standard of roles she was being asked to play, and eventually moved to London to escape the punitive (as she saw it) terms of the contract. The studio, Warner Bros, took exception, and applied for an injunction in the English courts to prevent her from committing any breach. The actress defended the case under her married name of Ruth Nelson, but by then was known to all by her stage name, which was composed of her childhood nickname followed by her maiden name: Bette Davis.

Her contract was in the standard form under the old Hollywood system, whereby actors would sign exclusive deals with one studio lasting a number of years. The contract further provided (in cl 23) that if at any time Davis refused to perform her services, the duration of the contract would be extended by such time as she spent acting the recalcitrant.

The downside in Davis's case was not the level of remuneration. By 1932, aged in her early 20s, she was reputedly earning $1,000 per week. Nor could it have been the absence of critical acclaim: she had been praised by reviews in *Life* magazine and the *New York Times*, and had received an Academy Award in 1935 for *Dangerous* (she would subsequently maintain that she had invented the nickname for the statue of "Oscar", but most film historians disagree). Despite all that, Davis firmly believed

Published in the *New Law Journal*, vol 162, 18 May 2012, p 690. With thanks to Guy Skelton for his assistance.

that her career was being blighted by only being offered mediocre roles, hence her flight to England.

In the previous case of *Gaumont-British Picture Corporation Ltd v Alexander* [1936] 2 All ER 1686, a similar contract had been held valid despite its highly restrictive terms. Davis therefore could not object to the contract *per se*. Nor could she dispute that she had breached its terms. Instead, she argued simply that the contract should not be enforced by way of injunction.

Leading counsel for Warner Bros was Sir Patrick Hastings KC. Something of a theatrical sort himself, one of his plays had been made into a silent film in 1927, though he (apparently wisely) did not give up his day job. He had gained more lasting fame as Attorney General during the time of the Campbell case in the mid-1920s which brought down the first Labour government (when it tried to interfere with the Attorney's independence by stopping a prosecution of certain members of the party).

In his opening speech Hastings submitted that Davis's case was about a "rather naughty lady". Referring to her reputed description of the contract's punitive terms as "slavery", he referred (incorrectly) to her salary being $1,350 per week and offered that

> "if anybody wants to put me into perpetual servitude on the basis of that remuneration, I shall prepare to consider it."

Hastings further submitted that Davis had the wit and ability to pursue a different career if she chose – a somewhat unrealistic comment in view of the limited career opportunities for women of the time. He concluded that "what she wants is more money".

That seemed to be the view of the press and indeed that of the judge, Branson J, who said that Davis's actions had "no discoverable reason, except that she wanted more money".

Not surprisingly, therefore, Branson J went on to rule in the studio's favour (see [1936] 3 All ER 160). He held that where the enforcement of negative covenants did not amount to a decree of the specific performance of the positive covenants, or to obliging the employee to remain idle or perform the positive covenants, they could be enforced by injunction.

Reflecting the equitable nature of the remedy, he further held that the granting of such an injunction was discretionary and should be limited to what was reasonable in all the circumstances. In Davis's case, he limited the injunction in area to the jurisdiction of the court, and in time to the duration of the contract or three years, whichever was shorter.

A few years after Davis's case, however, another screen legend, Olivia de Havilland, brought a legal challenge to her contract in California. She objected successfully to the studio's invocation of the equivalent of cl 23 in Davis's contract, because Californian labour law did not permit a contract for personal services to exceed seven years' duration. The resultant victory was seen as a major blow to the power of the studios, and the labour statute under which she had gained victory became known as "De Havilland's law". The old studio system as a whole was finished before the end of the 1940s, thanks to unrelated litigation, though of course Warner Bros survived nevertheless.

As for Davis herself, the defeat left her in severe financial difficulty and with no realistic option other than to return to America and resume her career. Once there, however, she went from strength to strength, winning her second Oscar for *Jezebel* in 1938 and receiving Oscar nominations for each of the next five years. By 1942 she was allegedly the highest paid woman in America. She was also the first woman to receive a lifetime achievement award from the American Film Institute. All of which, one imagines, was ample compensation for losing in court all those years earlier ...

6. A fugitive seeks justice

Not many film directors have an *oeuvre* as critically acclaimed as that of Roman Polanski, winner of Academy Awards for *Chinatown* and *The Pianist*. Even fewer could possibly have had as tragic and tumultuous a personal life. Polanski was a child survivor of the Holocaust, the most notorious act of genocide of the twentieth century. His pregnant wife Sharon Tate was killed by the Manson family in California at the end of the 1960s, in one of the most notorious murders of the twentieth century.

On top of all that, Polanski is also a criminal himself, having pleaded guilty in 1977 to a charge of statutory rape in California after having sex with a 13-year-old girl. He fled to France prior to sentencing and remains a fugitive from justice to the present day.

In 2002 he had occasion to return to the legal system when an article appeared in *Vanity Fair* magazine. The article was about a New York restaurant, and offered an anecdote about Polanski trying to seduce a young girl shortly after Sharon Tate's murder.

Not surprisingly Polanski took umbrage, and wished to bring proceedings in libel. There was one problem: American courts would not entertain an action whilst he was a fugitive. He did not wish to sue in France. Instead he became what the tabloids like to call a "libel tourist", by bringing the action in London. He was able to do so because there had been publication in Britain, albeit on a considerably lesser scale than in the US.

As with other cases of foreign litigants seeking to take advantage of Britain's claimant-friendly libel laws, there were some mutterings about Polanski's choice of jurisdiction. Such was not Polanski's concern; instead he had to deal with the question of giving evidence when Britain had an extradition treaty with the United States.

Published in the *New Law Journal*, vol 161, 9 December 2011, p 1714.

He therefore applied to give evidence by video link (pursuant to r 32.3 of the Civil Procedure Rules 1998).

At first instance, Eady J rather unsurprisingly viewed the reasons for the application as "unattractive". Nevertheless he went on to allow it: any prejudice would be to the defendant's advantage, not that of Polanski; the technology was good enough for cross examination to take place "as naturally and freely as when a witness is present in the court room"; and if the application were to be refused, Polanski's case would likely fail, allowing the defendant to get away with publishing a potentially serious libel. The defendant appealed.

In allowing the appeal, the Court of Appeal pointed out that Polanski had chosen to sue in England and was asking for the court to exercise its discretion in his favour – not for anything he was entitled to as of right. If he had been on the run from England, it would beggar belief that an English court would indulge him in the manner sought. It should make no difference that he committed a crime in another, friendly jurisdiction.

By a 3-2 majority, however, the House of Lords allowed Polanski's subsequent appeal (see *Polanski v Condé Publications Ltd* [2005] UKHL 10). They dealt with a few Aunt Sallies first: there was no challenge to jurisdiction by the defendant. There was no question of Polanski's fugitive status precluding him from bringing any action at all, since he had not thereby lost all his civil rights – it was not as if someone could steal the intellectual property of his films with impunity, for example. There was also no dispute that the court had power to allow the application.

For the majority, the decisive factor was that Polanski was entitled to the protection of the court of his civil rights notwithstanding his fugitive status. That being so, he should have recourse to one of the court's procedures, even those which enabled him to remain a fugitive whilst prosecuting the case. There was no logical reason why he should have the right to bring the action whilst a fugitive but not the facility to conduct it because he was a fugitive.

It is easy to see why the judges were sharply divided. On the one hand Polanski should not have had any assistance in evading justice. On the other hand he should not have been deprived of all his civil rights because of his fugitive status, nor should the defendant have gained an unjust windfall by being able to libel him with impunity.

I have finally been persuaded that the correct decision was made, partly on the reasoning of the majority but also because, for the jury, Polanski's evasion of justice would stand squarely against him. They would know why he was unable to attend in person. The gravitas of his fame and status as a leading filmmaker would not help him if they thought he had used it to avoid prison. He would not be able to deploy his celebrity status in person. Nor would his reputation for libel purposes be enhanced by his criminal record.

So the right result, if more than a shade tawdry, was reached in the end. And what happened next? Polanski went on to win the substantive action and was awarded over £50,000. In 2008, he went to Switzerland without realising it had an extradition treaty with the United States and was arrested, but to his considerable good fortune the Swiss declined the subsequent American extradition request and he was allowed to return to France, where he remains. He has continued to make feature films, and with a certain irony his 1977 conviction was the subject of a controversial documentary. It seems unlikely he will ever be one for a quiet life.

Part III: Law and War

This part of the book combines my lifelong hobby of military history with my day job in the law. Philosophically speaking, obviously enough, law and war are polar opposites: one involves the resolution of disputes by the non-violent application of rules known in advance and impartially administered; the other involves the resolution of disputes by killing human beings on an industrial scale.

Because of that diametric opposition, it is often said that the ultimate test of a legal system is whether and to what extent it maintains the rule of law during wartime – in the form of abiding by international law, restraining the conduct of its armed forces and maintaining the liberties of its citizens. These issues are explored in a number of the articles in this part.

To begin with, however, is a tale of a slightly different sort – the famous duel between the USS *Kearsarge* and the CSS *Alabama* off the coast of France during the American Civil War. There are many fascinating – and sobering – statistics about that conflict, aside from the fact that all of modern history would have been drastically different had the South prevailed. More Americans died in the war than in every other war America has fought combined. By its conclusion the North fielded the most powerful army in the world. The Northern navy might not have matched the Royal Navy of the day in global terms, but it could have made life very uncomfortable for it in the Atlantic. With that in mind, Britain was anxious to remain – and visibly remain – neutral, to the point where it chose a potentially highly expensive arbitration process rather than risk a clash of arms when the Americans demanded compensation for Britain having assisted the Southern navy.

Moving to the second great industrialised conflict, the Great War, we consider three quite different state executions. The first was the murder by the Germans of the British merchant naval captain Charles Fryatt, a despicable act that was not justifiable at the time and has only looked worse since.

Turning to the next case, in modern times the execution of Private Harry Farr by his own side in the same conflict has been argued by some as equally objectionable. The argument is based on the contention that Private Farr was an innocent victim of shellshock. In my view, however, for all the sympathy that Private Farr undoubtedly deserved, it is wrong for later generations to try to rewrite the military law of the desperate days of 1916. If Britain had not gone to war he would not have been executed, it is true, but it is not true to say that his execution was a random callous act or otherwise unlawful according to the law of the day.

Similar arguments to the case of Private Farr have been made about Roger Casement and William Joyce: it has been alleged that they were executed out of anti-Irish bigotry or anti-German revenge, or some other irrational or immoral motivation. Again I take the view that the circumstances of the time justified finding them guilty of treason, though as an opponent of the death penalty I would have opted for another form of punishment (as, for that matter, I would have in Private Farr's case).

With PG Wodehouse and Helen Duncan much might be said about the former's poor judgment and naivety and the latter's absurdity, but neither should have been considered a criminal. The prosecuting authorities therefore showed appropriate restraint in not attempting to charge Wodehouse, but frankly wasted their time and money in prosecuting Duncan. Both cases remain controversial – as recently as 2011 Wodehouse was in the news after files from MI6 were declassified. I saw no reason to alter my own view of the affair, but there were certainly those in the popular press who thought otherwise.

The time after the two world wars of the twentieth century is generally referred to the "post-war era". As an aside I would suggest that that should only refer to the period from 1945 to 1991 (the time of the first Gulf War) at the earliest, and until 1999 at the latest. Thereafter, until at least the time of writing, the most accurate description would be the "small-war era". Or at least it should be for Britain, whose troops have been deployed in at least one overseas engagement every year since.

As I have argued, the war against Serbia in 1999 seems largely – and wrongly – to have been forgotten. But the legality of the war was highly questionable, at least according to the Foreign Affairs Committee, which must constitute the authoritative voice of the nation on the issue. The Committee went on to brush that point aside and argued that the war was nonetheless morally justified. I would dispute that proposition, but either way it is hard to escape the conclusion that the fortuitous outcome of Kosovo had considerable bearing on the decision of the UK government to go to war with Iraq four years later, with all the consequences that that entailed.

The overarching conflict of the small-war era is the so-called "war on terror", which was used to justify the wars in both Afghanistan and Iraq. One domestic manifestation was the *Corner House* saga, in which a very substantial investigation of fraud on the part of a very significant British company was halted in its tracks by the intervention of one of the UK's chief allies, Saudi Arabia. The Saudis bluntly told the UK authorities that they would withdraw their co-operation in the "war on terror" unless the investigation was stopped. The implications for the rule of law in this country, not to say the sour moral taste, need no elaboration. But the world of realpolitik has always been morally dubious, and occasionally legally dubious as well, which is why it is called realpolitik in the first place.

Latest in the small wars has been the Libyan intervention in 2011. As of the time of writing, it seems to have been concluded more quickly and more successfully than Iraq or Afghanistan. Legally speaking, however, there remain serious unanswered questions, not least over the White House's position that the action did not constitute a "war", and it is still early days in terms of judging whether or not the new regime will have any time for the rule of law or human rights. Meanwhile things seem to be at least as bad in Syria, though there has been no serious call for intervention by British forces.

Finally in this part we return to an issue familiar to those of Private Farr's day, raising the issue of conscientious objection. It seems to me that in a volunteer army the case for recognising conscientious objection is very much less than under conscription.

I would note that there has not been occasion to consider a much broader issue, which is the often unstated – and certainly underrated – impact of war on the law in this country. It is often remarked how modern attitudes to individual liberty were shaped by the two world wars, and how both conflicts did for the class system. I would go much further and argue that nothing less than the whole *raison d'être* of the state itself – and the legal system with it – was fundamentally and irrevocably altered by the two world wars, as well as the Great Depression that fell between them.

In 1910 some 25% of state expenditure was on the navy. The welfare state was in its infancy, much of the country lived in abject poverty, industry was wholly privately owned and employment rights protection was minimal to say the least. It was because the state felt no option other than to commit itself to "total war" – where all economic activity was to be directed to the war effort – that it then intervened in so many aspects of life that had previously been thought none of its business. The modern regulatory state which is responsible for the enormous amount of legislation and regulation of the present day was thereby born.

The regulatory state was extended by the need to reprise total war in the Second World War, and extended further still by the need to rebuild the country afterwards. Two world wars had left the electorate demanding fundamental changes to society, reflected in the victory of Attlee's government with its programme of social reforms requiring unprecedented levels of state intervention. Our society would have been unimaginably different without the resultant changes.

7. A duel on the high seas: the Alabama claims

Lord Bingham (1933-2010) was perhaps the best known judge of his generation. Recently a second collection of his speeches and essays has been published (*Lives of the Law*, OUP, 2011). They cover a wide range of subjects, from legal history to human rights, politics and law. The inquiring mind will find something of interest in all of them. A good example is the chapter on the *Alabama* claims of 1871-2, a saga perhaps not as well known as Bingham seems to have assumed, but one which would prove revolutionary in legal terms.

The claims arose out of the great nineteenth-century clash of arms that was the American Civil War. From the outset the conflict was keenly observed in Europe – especially in Britain, where the events of 1776 and 1812 were still just about in living memory. It would have been plain by 1861 that the size of the United States would inevitably lead to a new, perhaps irresistible, power joining the great game. America could not easily be restrained by the European powers, but a civil war might do the trick for them.

Meanwhile, across the Atlantic, the Confederacy faced a daunting task. Outnumbered by 2:1 in population, and many times over in industrial capacity, it stood no chance of building a competitive navy by itself. Hopes that Britain or France might join the conflict proved groundless (despite Gladstone's unfortunate prediction of a Confederate triumph). There was, however, still the option for the Confederacy of purchasing ships from European yards.

In Britain they encountered a problem: s 7 of the Foreign Enlistment Act 1819, passed to keep British nationals out of South American colonial struggles with Spain, precluded British nationals arming or equipping any vessel within the jurisdiction for a foreign conflict.

It did not, however, prohibit the construction of a ship capable of being converted for warfare, provided that the conversion took place elsewhere. British shipbuilders exploited that lacuna to the fury of the Union and the consequent frustration of their own government. By such means the Confederacy acquired several fighting-standard ships, the most famous of which it renamed *Alabama*.

In June 1864 *Alabama* put into Cherbourg, following a prolific two-year campaign during which she had accounted for 64 Union vessels. The venue was chosen because it was reasoned that the French would be more sympathetic than the British, the latter having received searing epistles from the Union for supplying *Alabama* and similar vessels.

It was then that the drama properly began. The *Alabama*'s presence was discovered by the Northern warship USS *Kearsarge*, which promptly blockaded the port. News of the impending showdown spread amongst the *haute société* holidaying in the region. Opportunistic boat owners started offering tickets to would-be spectators. This was, after all, an age which did not shun bloodsports, and the warring Americans were about to produce a grand example. The respective commanders agreed battle in the manner of an old-fashioned duel, and *Alabama* steamed out of harbour to meet her fate. Among the spectators was the artist Edward Manet, who later produced a famous oil painting of the event (*Battle of Kearsage and Alabama*). There was also a British national on his private yacht, who had offered his sons a choice between observing the battle and attending church. The French authorities demanded that battle take place at least six miles offshore rather than the territorial three, because the range of both vessels' guns might otherwise reach land. They sent a gunboat out to act as a sort of linesman in that regard.

Rather as a microcosm of the war itself, *Alabama* had her moments, but eventually succumbed to her opponent's greater firepower. A year later the Confederacy went the same way, and the newly re-United States went looking for compensation from those who had backed the loser. Negotiations led to an international arbitration to determine whether Britain should be made to pay damages for the exploits of the *Alabama* and other ships. That was an extraordinary event because it involved the greatest power of its day voluntarily accepting a process which it knew could end badly – as indeed it did – rather than deflecting any complaint with the rattle of a sabre. Britain was ordered to pay $15.5m in gold, the significance of which is perhaps best expressed by the fact that it formed about 5% of her national budget at the time.

The settlement was not reached without some tortuous legal and political machinations, which Bingham describes in appropriate detail. Gladstone, on better form than with his earlier prediction, thought the award harsh, but "as dust in the balance" compared with the moral example of two nations choosing a judicial tribunal instead of the "arbitrament of the sword". That example began a process which culminated in modern institutions such as the International Court of Justice. It also did much to rebuild the relationship between Britain and America, though whether that deserved the epithet "special" was as debatable then as it is now. Over a century later, when the wreck was discovered, another precedent-setting international agreement on its ownership was formulated between the United States and France, given that it concerned an American vessel in French waters. Effectively ownership of the wreck was shared.

Tragically, however, the *Alabama* claims proved far less a portent than the Civil War itself, which formed a ringing demonstration of the consequences of warfare in the industrial age. Needless to say, in Europe and elsewhere, it fell on deaf ears.

8. Death of a civilian hero: the murder of Captain Charles Fryatt

During the course of the First World War British propaganda regularly alleged that German soldiers were committing atrocities in Belgium and occupied France. Debate has taken place ever since as to whether any of the macabre stories were true. Doubtless some, if not the majority, were exaggerated, though in recent years historians have tended to the view that there were indeed examples of appalling crimes being committed by German occupiers.

As it happens one shocking story is certainly true, not simply from independent evidence, but also avowed testimony from the German perpetrators themselves – who, rather than denying the incident, defiantly sought to justify their actions. It concerns the execution of the British Merchant Naval Captain Fryatt in 1916.

Charles Algernon Fryatt was born in 1872 and became a long-serving employee of the Great Eastern Railway Co. On the outbreak of war he held the rank of captain. His usual duties involved commanding vessels on return voyages from Harwich to Rotterdam. He continued to sail the same route after hostilities began, despite the rapidly increasing U-Boat threat. In March 1915, vessels under his command were subjected to three separate attacks, two of which would ultimately lead to his tragic place in history.

In the first incident, using deckhands to assist the stokers, he coaxed the ship SS *Wrexham* to two knots higher than her usual top speed, and thereby successfully evaded the chasing U-Boat for some 40 nautical miles before reaching the safety of Rotterdam. Fryatt was given a gold watch by the Great Eastern Railway Co with an enscription explaining that it was "a mark of their appreciation of his courage and skilful seamanship" during the incident.

The second event occurred on 28 March, when Fryatt was captain of SS *Brussels*. He was ordered to stop by a U-Boat near the Maas lightvessel, an area which saw much naval action during the war. Far from handing his vessel over, however, Fryatt took advantage of the inherent vulnerability of the U-Boat, which could only attack whilst on the surface. Rather like the fictional HMS *Thunderchild* in H.G. Wells' *War of the Worlds*, Fryatt proceeded at full steam ahead and tried to ram his attacker. The U-Boat managed to evade collision by crash-diving, but Fryatt was able to make good his escape as a result. Once again he was awarded a gold watch enscribed with a message of congratulation about his gallantry. On this occasion the gift was from the Admiralty, who also gave him a certificate printed on vellum, a material derived from animal skin which is still used today for an archival copy of every Act of Parliament. British propaganda also had a field day over the incident.

Fryatt's actions in confronting his aggressors had official approbation in the form of orders issued by the First Lord of the Admiralty, Winston Churchill. The orders constitute the first questionable legal aspect of the Fryatt saga, because they stipulated that U-Boat crews were to be considered felons rather than prisoners of war, and might be shot if it was not convenient to take them prisoner. All of that has an air of Admiral Sir Arthur Wilson's famous denunciation of submarines as "underhand, underwater and damned un-English". The existence of Churchill's orders came to the Germans' attention later in 1915 when they captured a vessel which was carrying a copy, and one can imagine their reaction.

In June 1916 Fryatt's luck finally ran out when his vessel *Brussels* was surrounded by five German destroyers. Although he managed to have all official papers destroyed before the vessel was taken into port, the Germans deduced who he was by the enscriptions on the two watches, which he had still been carrying. They then subjected him to a court martial. He was charged with being a *franc-tireur*, a term which originated in the 1870 Franco-Prussian war to describe irregular militia, but which the Germans used in the Great War to describe Belgian and French resistance, whom they regarded as "traitors". Fryatt was found guilty and sentenced to death. The sentence was confirmed by the Kaiser himself before being carried out by firing squad. An officious "execution notice" was issued afterwards by the German authorities, which asserted

> "The English captain ... though he did not belong to the armed forces of the enemy, attempted ... to destroy a German submarine by running it down. This is the reason why he has been condemned to death ... A perverse action has thus received its punishment, tardy but just".

Not surprisingly the British were outraged. Neutral states joined in the condemnation as well, the Swiss *Journal de Geneve* for example stating that

> "It is monstrous to maintain that armed forces have a right to murder civilians but that civilians are guilty of a crime in defending themselves".

Nevertheless, after the war a German International Law Commission, headed by Walter Schucking, issued a curt – though not unanimous – judgment concluding that Fryatt's execution "contains no violation of international law". General Ludendorff, German commander on the Western front, also wrote a post-bellum memoir in which he attempted to defend the general policy of executing *franc-tireurs*.

Ludendorff's apologia was swiftly shot down by, among others G K Chesterton, who memorably described it as the view of a "lurid and lamentable fool". It is hard to disagree, though it should be said that Ludendorff had clearly suffered a breakdown towards the end of the war and, despite a partial recovery, was presumably not of entirely sound mind thereafter.

Herr Schucking, on the other hand, was a distinguished scholar who went on to become Germany's first judge at the International Court of Justice. And yet his argument in respect of Fryatt was as intellectually dismal as Ludendorff's. Even if Churchill's orders on the treatment of German submariners (not a point relied on by

Schucking) went too far in seeking to classify submariners as illegitimate soldiers, there is the simple cliché that two wrongs don't make a right. No recrimination would have followed for the commander of the U-Boat had he sunk SS *Brussels* instead. It is therefore a perversion of logic to suggest that Fryatt could render himself a criminal by defending himself against the possibility.

International law, for most of its history at least, has been a protean concept, often conforming to the old Marxist description of "politics by another name". But few other than Schucking have ever argued that any permissible interpretation would have justified the execution of Fryatt for attempting to evade capture by enemy forces. Unarmed civilians should not be transformed into soldiers, let alone war criminals deserving the death penalty, simply by acting in self-defence when threatened by the enemy.

At the very most an argument could have been made that by his actions Fryatt had made himself a combatant, but in that case upon his capture he should have been treated as an ordinary prisoner of war, not a category of persons who were executed as a matter of routine.

To place the matter in context, both the German atrocity and Churchill's earlier orders reflect the importance – and hence desperation – of the U-Boat battle. Almost from the outset it was recognised as one of the battlefields that could determine the entire war on its own, as it was to be in the Second World War as well. It should be unarguable though that even the highest stakes do not excuse the murder of a civilian, and certainly not a captured individual who poses no further threat.

I am relieved to add, however, that if there was a tragic end to Fryatt's life there was at least a happy coda. He was posthumously awarded the Belgian Order of Leopold and the Belgian Maritime War Cross. The Netherlands Chapter of the League of Neutral States created a memorial tablet of marble and bronze which to this day stands in Liverpool St station in London. Fryatt's widow received a pension of £250 per annum from his employer and a lump sum of £300 from his insurers, as well as a personal letter of condolence from George V.

After the war, Fryatt's body was exhumed and returned to England, where a major service was held at St Paul's. Recognition extended to Canada, where two mountains, Mt Fryatt and Brussels Peak, were named in honour of Fryatt and his ship respectively.

Decades on, Fryatt's memory has largely faded from public conscience, but the generosity and memorials which followed mean that for his widow at least – unlike the majority of other widows or veteran soldiers – the country after the war was indeed a land fit for heroes. Sadly his murder was not the first or last case in which the perpetrators tried to dress it up as a legally justifiable action. International law remains something of a shifting sand, though I hope that by now it has managed a consensus that captured civilians should not be executed.

9. Shot at dawn: the court martial of Private Harry Farr

"... the hand of Time rested on the half-hour mark, and all along that old front line of the English there came a whistling and a crying. The men of the first wave climbed up the parapets, in tumult, darkness, and the presence of death, and having done with all pleasant things, advanced across No Man's Land to begin the Battle of the Somme."

John Masefield, *The Old Front Line*, 1917

Introduction

At first light on 16 October 1916, Private Harry Farr of the 1st Battalion, the West Yorkshire Regiment, was led by his colleagues into a forest in the region of the Somme River in France. The eponymous allied offensive, the most bloody battle of the most bloody war in British history, was nearing its end. For all the blood spilt, the achievement of the battle had been limited to say the least: little ground had been gained, the general stalemate would thereafter resume, and the war would not be over for another two years and several million more deaths.

Private Farr would live to see none of that, for he was being taken into the woods that day for his own execution, having been found guilty of failing to take his place in the front line. It is, one might reasonably suggest, fairly safe to assume that no-one present at Private Farr's trial or execution would have even begun to imagine that almost ninety years later his daughter would be in attendance at the Royal Courts of Justice on the Strand to hear a judicial review of their actions. Nor would they have anticipated that Parliament would cut the litigation short by issuing a blanket pardon for Private Farr and all others executed for cowardice or related crimes in the Great War. Still less would they have imagined that Private Farr would have a Myspace page devoted to him.

All those things did come to pass, however, and thus in 2006 the trial of Private Harry Farr came to public attention as a reminder of the small part he played in the conflict which inflicted incalculable misery on the nations involved and changed all of them forever.

The nature of the war

To understand properly the circumstances under which Private Farr's trial and sentence were undertaken, it is necessary to say something of the nature of the war itself. The British army during the war faced a task of extraordinary complexity and difficulty, for which it was almost completely unprepared. It had spent the previous century planning to avoid another European land conflict and instead rely on the navy as the country's primary contribution and the guarantee of its own safety. It made many mistakes, some of calamitous proportions. And yet it was the only army engaged throughout the war which did not suffer a collapse at any point as well, of course, as emerging victorious. Moreover, by 1918 it had become the most powerful field army in the world – the only time in history that it has qualified for that description.

Two points follow. First, the popular image of the generals in charge of this process as nothing more than bungling butchers, "donkeys leading lions", is not sustainable in the face of the army's ultimate achievement, for all the undoubtedly serious mistakes they made in the process. Secondly, to expect military justice to achieve the same standard in the ghastly circumstances of 1914-18 as in peacetime is simply not realistic.

Civilian life in the 1910s also requires mention. The understanding and ethos of what modern readers would call health and safety, employment rights and the welfare state were very different from that of twenty-first century Britain. Life expectancy was far shorter. The soldiers who fought the Great War were born in Victorian times, and their attitudes to duty and character corresponded. The death penalty was the mandatory punishment for civilian murder and a possible punishment for a number of other offences as well.

It follows that it cannot be assumed that the majority of civilians or soldiers at the time would have viewed the execution of soldiers for cowardice (or any other crime) in anything like the same way as those in the present day might.

Private Farr's war

Harry Farr enters the story of the Great War at the beginning, volunteering for the British Expeditionary Force in 1914. There is no dispute that he was subjected to shell fire, and that he had spent some time out of the trenches as a result. Eventually, in September 1916, he told a Regimental Sergeant Major that he "could not stand it". The response was Victorian in its message, but decidedly un-Victorian in its language: "You are a fucking coward and you will go to the trenches. I give fuck all for my life and I give fuck all for yours and I'll get you fucking well shot". Still Farr refused, and later broke away from his escorts on the way to the front. He was arrested and charged with showing cowardice in the face of the enemy.

At the subsequent court martial Farr did not deny the above sequence of events. He offered by way of explanation only that "being away from the shell fire I felt better". Almost certainly that sealed his fate. The inevitable verdict was guilty and the customary sentence was death.

The aftermath

Private Farr's family kept the manner of his death as a shameful secret for years afterwards. It was not until the government's decision in 1992 to lift the classification of the relevant surviving documents for all the executed soldiers that a public campaign began in earnest to clear his name.

The government of the day refused, as did the new Labour government in 1997, although the latter did declare that the men shot at dawn were as much victims of the conflict as anyone else. Private Farr's relatives remained dissatisfied and in March 2006, all other avenues having failed, they appeared in the High Court seeking judicial review of the refusal to grant a pardon. Parliament was spurred into action and, following an adjournment of the proceedings, responded with the final act in the legal saga, s 359 of the Armed Forces Act 2006.

It was freely acknowledged in the House that the inherent difficulties in the issue rendered the solution a compromise. The section stated that anyone executed for offences such as cowardice was "taken to be pardoned", with the qualifications that no individual soldier's conviction or sentence was overturned and no surviving relatives or anyone else was to be given any compensation.

The pardon: right or wrong?

It may well be that the modern army would not have convicted some of those shot at dawn, because of a better understanding of shellshock and a different attitude to its sufferers. But that is not really the point. How can it be right for a generation which had not known the horrors of the First World War to be casting judgement on that which did? The courts martial should be seen in the context of the extraordinary crisis that the British Army faced, and if there is to be judgement with hindsight, it surely has to include the knowledge that the British Army eventually won.

Moreover, it cannot be too callous logic to argue that judicial and Parliamentary resources should be prioritised for the living and to allow the rights and wrongs of the past to remain the preserve of historians.

It is not as though the offences themselves were contrary to modern morals: the crimes of desertion and cowardice remained just as much a part of military law in 2006 as in 1916. The main objection to the courts martial verdicts therefore has to be the correctness of the individual convictions – which Parliament itself regularly found impossible to judge given the paucity of surviving evidence – or the use of the death penalty (the public campaign used the phrase "shot at dawn" not "convicted of cowardice or desertion").

The prior objections of the state to a pardon had focused primarily on the quality of evidence, and those objections were never fully answered. Indeed, they were cited as a reason for the pardon in the watered-down form it eventually appeared. Whatever the qualifications in the 2006 Act, however, the reality was and remains that most of the lay public would read the granting of the pardon as being exculpatory of the executed.

Some 5.7 million served in the British Army during the Great War and it would be statistically improbable for there to have been no instances of cowardice or desertion amongst them. The authorities of the day decided that there had been approximately 3,000 such instances, but applied the ultimate sanction only to 10% of them (the rest had their sentences commuted). That seems less arbitrary and cruel than humane. Indeed, the statistics point to an unknown and unknowable further probability. More than 80,000 veterans were diagnosed with shell shock after the war. One can assume therefore that there must have been thousands of instances of minor shell shock, the sufferers of which did not actually become recorded casualties. Some would have become disorientated for a short while at least, and been separated from their units. Technically they would have been deserters. And yet what must have happened on many such occasions (for, if it had not, there would have been far more prosecutions than there were in fact) is that sympathetic soldiers from other units would have ushered the men back to their own units, where they would have been received without too many questions being asked.

Obviously the soldiers who carried out the courts martial could not defend their name, since by 2006 all involved had died and the majority never spoke of the events.

Finally, we return to the fundamental objection: the pardon was imposing a judgment on men who were not there to defend their actions, who acted in circumstances which the people of 2006 never knew for themselves, and who were prosecuting acts which remain military offences to the present day. We should not pass judgement on them.

10. Be careful what you wish for: Abu Hamza, Sir Roger Casement and William Joyce

The radical Muslim cleric Abu Hamza has won his recent appeal against the attempt by British authorities to strip him of his passport. Having already lost his Egyptian nationality, he argued successfully that removing his British passport would render him stateless.

It seems rather incongruous that Hamza wanted a British passport at all, given his reported attitude towards the British state. He might remember the old adage about being careful what you wish for: the last person to engage in claiming a British passport then trying to bring about the downfall of the state was the rather colourful William Joyce, better known as the wartime traitor Lord Haw Haw.

Joyce was a member of several different British fascist political parties during the 1920s and 30s (they tended to splinter and reform in a manner similar to Monty Python's Judean parties in *Life of Brian*). As war with Germany loomed, Joyce, fearing internment, applied successfully to renew his British passport in order to flee the country.

Upon arriving in Berlin he soon began broadcasting propaganda for Nazi radio. Throughout the war he taunted the British over the airways about the bombing of their cities and constantly urged them to surrender. In June 1945 he was captured and charged with three counts of high treason.

There was one problem: Joyce was not actually British. He was born in America, of Irish descent. Two of the counts therefore fell away on the ground that as a foreign national he had not owed allegiance to the Crown.

Published in *Criminal Law & Justice Weekly*, vol 174, 27 November 2010, p 249.

Joyce was, however, convicted on the count relating to the period of his broadcasting in which he had held a valid British passport (which had lapsed in 1940). The courts reasoned that since he had enjoyed the protection that that document conferred, had used it to travel and could have used it in a neutral state, he owed reciprocal obligations to the Crown during the period of its validity, notwithstanding that he hadn't strictly been entitled to it in the first place.

His conviction was not without controversy, but it is hard to see any moral objection. Joyce had deceived the British authorities into thinking he was a British citizen when it suited him. He should have realised that they might go along with that pretence when it suited them. He fully deserved to come unstuck on that one.

In the years since, Joyce's apologists have suggested he was executed out of revenge, or prejudice against his Irish origins.

Revenge is a distasteful motive, although it is easy for those who did not live through the terror of the Blitz to say so. As to the second point, Joyce was an ardent unionist who claimed to have fled Ireland to escape assassination by the IRA, making him a curious candidate for martydom in the cause of Irish independence.

Once it had been established that Joyce owed allegiance to the Crown for a certain period, then it did not matter that his impugned acts had been committed outside the jurisdiction, in the light of a case from the previous war involving another famous traitor, Sir Roger Casement.

Casement's history was if anything more colourful than Joyce's. He had gained fame, and a knighthood, for exposing colonial depredations in Africa and South America. Upon returning to the UK, he aligned himself with the cause of Irish nationalism. During the Great War he attempted (without much success) to obtain material support from Germany for an Irish uprising. He was caught and charged with treason on his return to the UK.

Casement's defence argued that all of his impugned acts had taken place on German soil. That was deemed irrelevant on the court's interpretation of the Treason Act 1351, which defined treason as giving the King's enemies "aid and comfort in the realm, or elsewhere"; "elsewhere" being defined as elsewhere than the jurisdiction.

That ruling was also not without controversy but, as with Joyce, the moral position seems clear, leaving aside the merits of Casement's cause of Irish independence, the mitigation of his good work in Africa and the Americas, and the still unresolved "black diaries" controversy (wherein he was alleged to have been involved in what in modern terms would be called predatory sex tourism). Someone leaving the jurisdiction, plotting to overthrow the state and then returning should not expect the state to find itself powerless to respond.

Since then the law of treason seems to have fallen into disuse, with no prosecutions since Joyce's, despite a number of apparently qualifying individuals. The authorities seem to prefer other charges. The offence remains on the statute books, however, and if the likes of Hamza persist in their ways it might pay the Crown Prosecution Service to reconsider its use. Nowadays inflammatory speech might find a defence based on Art 10 of the European Convention on Human Rights, but other treasonous activities, such as raising funds to support Britain's enemies, would not.

11. An innocent abroad: the non-trial of PG Wodehouse

Having just recounted two famous cases of wartime treason, we now turn to a famous case of non-treason from the Second World War. It involved one of England's greatest ever authors and is a lesson in overreaction, though ultimately a correct case of legal inaction.

In early 1940, as Panzer divisions smashed through the Low Countries and into France, it need hardly be said that most of Britain would have followed the news with close attention and a mixture of anxiety and horror. Not so, it would appear, a 58 year old Englishman living in the south of France, where he had resided for tax reasons since 1934. PG Wodehouse paid such little heed to world events that not even news of the atrocious events unfolding a few hundred miles away in the same country prompted him to flee before occupying German troops arrived. Shortly after the Vichy regime was formed, Wodehouse found himself interned along with all other British nationals in France.

In 1941, realising how naive and harmless he was, the Nazis let him go shortly before he was due to be released in any event (upon reaching the age of 60), but at the same time co-opted his naivety for some light-hearted radio broadcasts to America, which was still a neutral party at the time. Wodehouse accepted because he wanted to show some gratitude for the correspondence he had received from American fans during his internment.

To a modern audience, the broadcasts come across as politically irrelevant as they were irreverent; no more than light-hearted Wodehousian banter about barren towns, inept guards and the probable need to take a letter of introduction if he finally got to see his wife again. To a wartime audience in Britain, however, they were nothing

Published in *Criminal Law & Justice Weekly*, vol 174, 18 December 2010, p 791.

of the sort. Instead they were sufficiently offensive to have Wodehouse debated as a possible traitor in the House of Commons, and to have him specifically likened to Lord Haw Haw.

A number of public figures and institutions joined the attack, including the author AA Milne. Others came to Wodehouse's defence, including George Orwell and Evelyn Waugh. Thus arose perhaps the most surreal literary showdown in English history: the genial and unworldly Winnie the Pooh taking shots at the equally genial and unworldly Bertie Wooster, with Lord Sebastian Flyte and Winston Smith appearing for the defence.

One supposes Bertie Wooster might have gone pheasant shooting with Flyte in the Hundred Acre Wood, though Smith would have been denied any comparable pleasures in 1984. One also supposes that the denizens of Animal Farm were likely a more formidable lot than the gentle creatures of the Hundred Acre Wood …

In the event, no charges were ever brought and a consensus emerged that Wodehouse was wholly innocent. The affair had a terrible irony, however, given that just about the only overt political reference in any of Wodehouse's pre-war works was the character Roderick Spode, a direct satire of Oswald Mosley. It left a sad legacy too: Wodehouse never returned to England.

The story is a salutary reminder that one can go too far in the most worthy of causes. Obviously it was right that people did not want to give Nazi Germany a crumb of comfort in 1941. But, properly understood, Wodehouse's broadcasts gave no such crumb, or even a speck. Nor does that conclusion require hindsight, still less any Orwellian rewrite of history. Anyone familiar with Wodehouse's works – as most educated Englishmen were at the time – and the man himself, would have seen the innocent naivety for what it was.

One finds some mild parallels today, without drawing too long a bow. One recalls Paul Chambers' tweet in frustration at thwarted weekend plans that he would blow up an airport. It seems absurd that anyone would think his post a serious statement of terrorist intent. And yet Chambers found himself fined under the Communications Act 2003. It is telling that there were much more severe crimes with which Chambers could and should have been charged (but was not) had anyone actually taken him seriously. *

A second recent incident concerned Councillor Gareth Compton, who was incensed by the columnist Yasmin Alibhai-Brown's statement that Western politicians had no moral right to object to the stoning of a woman in Iran. Mr Compton tweeted that he wished someone would stone Alibhai-Brown to death instead. He was promptly arrested for his trouble.

Compton was released without charge, but it beggars belief that anyone would think he was actually advocating the act rather than making an attempt at sardonic humour.

Neither tweeter was particularly funny, still less Wodehousean. But nor should they have attracted the attention of the police, any more than Wodehouse should have been pilloried in public. Combating terrorism and maintaining community harmony requires acute judgement on the authorities' part, and the ability to recognise real threats. Equally it requires the ability to recognise blatant non-threats. Retaining a sense of humour wouldn't hurt in that regard.

* Chambers' conviction was eventually quashed by the High Court: see *Criminal Law & Justice Weekly*, vol 176, 22 September 2012, pp556-7

12. Witchcraft during wartime: the trial of Helen Duncan

The previous article concluded that PG Wodehouse was rightly never brought to trial for his actions in the Second World War. Here is a case which was, but should never have been: that of Helen Duncan, often (incorrectly) said to be the last person in Britain to be tried for witchcraft.

Duncan held herself out to be a spiritual medium. She received minor convictions for fraudulent activities relating to her "trade" before the Second World War, but acquired lasting fame during the conflict by telling one anguished person during a séance in late 1941 that her son's ship, HMS *Barham*, had been sunk.

News of this revelation caused alarm in Whitehall. The *Barham* had indeed been lost, but the Navy had suppressed the information. The reason was that intelligence had revealed that the Germans did not know about the sinking, since the U-Boat commander responsible had been unsure. Several other capital ships had been lost around the same time, and news of the *Barham*'s loss would have been a severe blow to morale as well as a German propaganda victory. Fearing that Duncan had access to its secrets, therefore, the state decided to put her out of business.

After some impressive pre-internet legal research by the prosecution, Duncan was charged under s 4 of the Witchcraft Act 1735, concerning "fraudulent spiritual activity" (rather than witchcraft per se). The trial that followed veered towards farce, with a number of apparently respectable people prepared to testify that her powers were genuine, but with the judge prohibiting Duncan herself from "proving" her abilities in court. She was eventually convicted by a jury and imprisoned for nine months.

Published in *Criminal Law & Justice Weekly*, vol 175, 15 January 2011, p 27.

After the trial Churchill lambasted the case as "tomfoolery", and it is hard to disagree. It seems absurd that the authorities thought Duncan either a genuine medium or privy to state secrets: the fact that she guessed that a ship during wartime had been sunk hardly constitutes proof of anything.

If Duncan had indeed improperly obtained state secrets, she should have been charged on those grounds accordingly. If that was the true reason for the trial, however, but the prosecution chose instead to prosecute her under the Witchcraft Act for its own convenience, then that looks like a misuse of the legal system.

The most persuasive ground for the law's intervention was that Duncan was exploiting the vulnerable, and that argument of course applies to all others in her vocation. There is clearly some justification for the state prosecuting charlatans. Then again, if people derive comfort from falsity, why should others object? In a free society, if competent adults wish to pay for such "services" they should have the right to do so, both as an exercise of the right to freedom of contract and the right to freedom of religion.

On the other hand, trading standards usually require that vendors do not offer for sale something they know to be false, particularly when the prospective purchaser is likely to be vulnerable.

In the absence of blatant trickery, however, the question of proof in either direction is an interesting one; after all, a good many intelligent people seem to want to believe in the Loch Ness monster, and it is not as if the veracity of mainstream religion is any more open to scientific proof. In all seriousness, the state is generally best leaving such things to the marketplace of ideas.

At most, spiritual mediums and similar types should be the concern of trading standards rather than the criminal law. There may come a point where coercion or deception merits criminal proceedings, but existing laws against intimidation or fraud should suffice in those cases. Otherwise, commercial regulation rather than specific criminal offences should be the extent of the law's intervention, the aim being to restrict misleading advertising or otherwise protect the vulnerable rather than shut down the business altogether.

The justification is that the state should adhere strictly to the separation of church and state. On the one hand, the state should not seek to outlaw peddlers of religion and spiritualism. On the other hand, no funding or official sanction should be given for spiritual or religious activities, "mainstream" or otherwise. Rather, the state should concentrate on education, surely the consumers' best weapon against snake oil salesmen of any kind.

Coda: Recently, supporters of Duncan campaigned to have her pardoned. They were unsuccessful, though their website seeks to assure everyone that Duncan's powers were genuine. Readers can judge that one for themselves.

13. Military history on trial

Early in 2000 an action was brought by one of the most unpopular and controversial professional authors in modern history, the *soi-disant* military historian David Irving, against the publisher Penguin Books. It finished with one of the most interesting and compellingly written judgments in all of the law reports, which remains required reading for anyone interested in the history of the Third Reich.

Irving's background was not as an academic historian. He attended university for a short time but left without any qualifications. He later went to Germany where he was employed as a steel worker. Whilst there he learned German and became interested in German history. Beginning in the 1960s he published a number of books on the Third Reich. Some of the early ones received a respectable amount of critical praise, such as *The Destruction of Dresden* (1963) and *Hitler's War* (1977). When the *Hitler Diaries* controversy arose in the 1980s Irving quickly denounced them as a hoax, but then wavered in his views for a time, leading others to quip that he might have been the first to say that they were a hoax but was also the last to maintain that they were genuine.

Irving became chiefly known for publications which downplayed the conventional view as to the extent – and at times even the existence – of the Holocaust, as well as the activities of Hitler and the Nazi regime in general. His critical and commercial success declined in parallel, leading (one infers) to something of a desperate move on his part at the turn of the century by resorting to challenging his critics in the libel courts rather than by the ordinary scholarly route of publishing counter-arguments in the form of books or articles.

The particular action he brought concerned a book by the American academic Deborah Lipstadt called *Denying the Holocaust – The Growing Assault on Truth and Memory*. Irving, representing himself, alleged that the book contained a number of defamatory meanings. The judge, Gray J, a veteran of the libel courts, found the following meanings proved: that Irving was an apologist for and partisan of Hitler, who had resorted to the distortion of evidence in order to serve his own purpose of exonerating Hitler and portraying him as sympathetic towards the Jews; that Irving was one of the most dangerous spokespersons for Holocaust denial; that Irving, in denying that the Holocaust happened, had bent or distorted historical evidence; and that he was discredited as an historian.

It therefore fell to be determined whether the allegations in those meanings were justified, for which the burden lay on the defendants. The judge said this of his task (para 1.3):

> "Needless to say, the context in which these issues fall to be determined is one which arouses the strongest passions. On that account, it is important that I stress at the outset of this judgment that I do not regard it as being any part of my function as the trial judge to make findings of fact as to what did and what did not occur during the Nazi regime in Germany. It will be necessary for me to rehearse, at some length, certain historical data. The need for this arises because I must evaluate the criticisms of or (as Irving would put it) the attack upon his conduct as an historian in the light of the available historical evidence. But it is not for me to form, still less to express, a judgement about what happened. That is a task for historians."

Having expressed that qualification, however, assessing and making statements of fact about incidents during the Nazi regime was precisely what the judge went on to do. Indeed he could not properly have disposed of the case otherwise. For example, he had to review considerable evidence, including expert testimony, concerning Auschwitz, in respect of which he wrote:

> "My overall assessment of the totality of the evidence that Jews were killed in large numbers in the gas chambers at Auschwitz is that it would require exceedingly powerful reasons to reject it."

He then considered Irving's counterarguments and concluded that they fell far short of disproving that evidence. He followed a similar process with similar results for other matters including Hitler's trial in 1924, Kristallnacht, the knowledge of Third Reich officials of the Holocaust and their participation therein, the shooting of the Jews in Riga, the bombing of Dresden, Hitler's own attitude to the Jews, and the Holocaust itself. In each instance he reviewed extensive evidence supporting the received view of events and compared it with Irving's offerings.

His verdict was clear and damning:

> "The charges which I have found to be substantially true include the charges that Irving has for his own ideological reasons persistently and deliberately misrepresented and manipulated historical evidence; that for the same reasons he has portrayed Hitler in an unwarrantedly favourable light, principally in relation to his attitude towards and responsibility for the treatment of the Jews; that he is an active Holocaust denier; that he is anti-semitic and racist and that he associated with right wing extremists who promote neo-Nazism. ..."

Irving's case accordingly failed. The judgment (*Irving v Penguin Books Ltd* [2000] All ER (D) 523) was subsequently published by Penguin in book form, unamended and without annotation. As mentioned, it makes for compelling reading. Ironically, therefore, it might be said that Irving finally managed to contribute to a well-received work on the Third Reich after all ...

Irving was refused permission to appeal (see [2001] All ER (D) 275 (Jul)). Although as a litigant in person he did not have legal representatives of his own to pay, the defendants were awarded their own (very substantial) costs, and they later brought a bankruptcy petition against him (see [2002] All ER (D) 313 (May)). Like many an unworthy claimant before him, Irving reaped what he sowed.

It follows that justice was unquestionably done. Yet one is left with a final, if moderate, sense of regret: it seems a waste that an historian of Irving's undoubted potential turned into such a scurrilous purveyor of untruths – let alone untruths told by way of trying to salvage the reputation of the most reviled regime in Western history. There was no disagreement at court that Irving had amassed a substantial amount of knowledge of the events of the Third Reich, and that he had done so by a lot of original research using primary sources. Had he not been blinded by bigotry, he would almost certainly have acquired a positive reputation as an historian and made a tangible contribution.

On the other hand, he only had himself to blame, and his reputation (along with his finances) was left where it belonged, and where it still remains: in tatters.

14. Lawyers, guns and money

The Bribery Act 2010 received Royal Assent on 8 April 2010. According to the Ministry of Justice, it will, among other things "provide a more effective legal framework to combat bribery in the public or private sectors" and "help tackle the threat that bribery poses to economic progress and development around the world".

It is fair to say that the old regime was a fractured state of affairs, and it is also fair to say that it didn't achieve very much. In 2007, for example, the US brought 69 cases relating to foreign bribery, Germany 43 and the UK none at all.

It cannot be said, therefore, that there was no case for reform. If anything the surprise is the length of time reform has taken; it is not as if the previous government was reticent about altering the criminal law in any other respect. The total number of pages in *Halsbury's Statutes* devoted to criminal law more than doubled between 1997 and 2010. That sort of increase is totally inconsistent with the rule of law, which requires, among other things, the law to be reasonably stable and knowable in advance.

Justified or not, it may be doubted whether the new Act will have the desired effect. The fact that the old law was in a slightly jaded state can scarcely be a complete explanation for the dearth of successful prosecutions. Perhaps the most famous, or rather infamous, case of a non-prosecution was the Al Yamamah investigation of the mid-2000s by the Serious Fraud Office (SFO).

Readers may recall that the investigation concerned the sale of Eurofighter jets to Saudi Arabia. The director of the SFO formed the view that there had been fraud, and began an investigation accordingly. All proceeded as normal until BAE Systems plc (the Eurofighter's manufacturer) said that to comply with a notice for disclosure would impair relations between Britain and Saudi Arabia. That

Published in the *New Law Journal*,vol 160, 12 November 2010, p1572 initially did not suffice to prevent the investigation, but in short order the Saudis upped the stakes. They made quite clear that unless the investigation was halted two things would follow: first, the Eurofighter deal (and presumably any future weapons purchase) would be called off; and secondly, co-operation in the "war on terror" would cease. In case anyone didn't get the hint, the implications of the second threat were spelt out—British lives on British streets would be put at risk. And just to make sure the right people heard, they made those threats directly to No. 10 Downing Street (not being convinced of the constitutional arrangement of the independence of the prosecution process in Britain).

By means of a "Shawcross exercise" the Attorney General (who superintends the Director as with every other prosecutorial authority) had solicited the views of the cabinet in relation to the implications for foreign relations and, given the unambiguous threat emanating from Riyadh, ultimately concluded that it was not in the public interest to continue with the investigation, much less prosecute anyone.

That decision was the subject of well-known judicial review proceedings (*R (on the application of Corner House Research) v Director of the Serious Fraud Office* [2008] 4 All ER 927), but despite the Divisional Court railing against what it saw as an abominable interference with the rule of law, on appeal the House of Lords gave the complaints short shrift. Distasteful as it all was, their lordships held the decision of the Director was not unlawful by traditional judicial review criteria, and therefore could not be interfered with by the courts. He had been entitled to take into account the public interest, in particular the threat to British lives, and indeed could have reached no other decision in the circumstances of the case.

One can look at the Al Yamamah affair from several different angles: a supine capitulation in the face of a foreign threat (that would presumably have set Lord Palmerston spinning in his grave), or a correct utilitarian balancing of the public interest. Or an outrageous selling out of the rule of law versus a proper exercise of the discretion which the prosecuting authorities have always correctly possessed. One thing, however, seems clear beyond argument: no matter what the state of the bribery laws, the Attorney General (or his subordinates) will exercise the discretion not to prosecute when they conclude it is not in the UK's interest to do so. And when British lives are at stake they will inevitably follow that course.

It would therefore pay to bear in mind that although the bribery laws may have changed—the "war on terror" continues unabated; the state of the nation's finances has become worse; we are still committed to a costly and protracted armed struggle in Afghanistan; our planned weapons procurement programmes are in a shaky state; which means the defence industry is as well; and we are as dependent on foreign oil as ever. In those circumstances it seems most improbable that nothing resembling the Al Yamamah deal will happen again or that, if it does, it will be treated any differently.

Afterword

The underlying problem in the *Corner House* litigation was the state of the defence procurement industry and its importance to the nation in economic terms. On 22 September 2009 I had the following letter published in the *Times* on the point:

Sir,

> The first and last consideration in defence procurement (letters, Sept 18) should be obtaining the best quality equipment for our Forces given the resources available, not in providing a substitute for unemployment benefit for the incumbent government's marginal constituencies. I would far rather have to inform a factory worker that he or she is being made redundant than have to explain to a soldier's parents that their child has been killed because of inadequate equipment. That it has taken four decades to produce a worthy partly British-built combat jet is an argument against, not for, attempting any such folly in future.

> The only actual combat role that it is possible to conceive the Eurofighter undertaking is that of supporting ground troops against insurgents. Such a role can be carried out more effectively — and cheaply — by drones and attack helicopters.
>
> Strategic bombing would be more effective, cheaper, and far less risky to personnel if undertaken by cruise missiles (or stealth aircraft, which the Eurofighter is not) rather than by conventional fast jets.
>
> The US military budget exceeds the next largest by a factor virtually unprecedented in history, and the cost-effectiveness of purchasing American equipment often corresponds. Further, there is no chance of Britain undertaking significant combat operations without at least some American equipment and assistance or — it might as well be conceded — political approbation.

Needless to say that was hoping against hope. It simply defies realpolitik to assume that those in Westminster and Whitehall will be able to ignore the vested interests of domestic arms manufacturers, even during wartime (and Britain has been engaged in war continuously for over a decade at the time of writing, indeed often more than one war at a time).

For the true scale of wastage and wasted opportunities in British defence procurement, one only needs to compare Britain and several other countries, most notably Israel, in terms of (i) the overall defence budget and the size of the forces each acquires; (ii) the ratio of the respective air forces' ground crew to aircraft; and (iii) the number of civil servants in each country working in the procurement field in the respective countries. The budget is similar, but the Israeli equipment is more numerous and effective; they have about half the number of ground staff per fast jet; and they also have a fraction of the number of procurement staff. (Note: for the avoidance of doubt, I am expressing no view – positive or negative – on Israel's use of its military.) France, too, manages to acquire more equipment than Britain with a similar budget (more nuclear warheads, fast jets, and indeed the total number of servicemen and women under arms).

Unless Britain's shabby history of military procurement is changed, the motivation to sell our equipment whenever and wherever we can, with the temptation to turn a blind eye to the consequences, will be undiminished. That does not mean we should have no defence industry – on the contrary, it should be an integral part of the country's manufacturing policy – but it has to be run properly.

15. A missed opportunity: the Chilcott Inquiry

The Chilcott Inquiry into the Iraq War has now heard its two star witnesses, the Prime Minister and his immediate predecessor, though we have not been promised a report before the end of this year. Already at least two questions of particular interest to lawyers have been raised, one procedural and one substantive.

The procedural issue is whether or not counsel to the inquiry should have been appointed. Obviously it is right that the panel should be primarily composed of military and political experts. But I do not think it is merely pushing the profession's barrel to suggest that the addition of senior counsel would have aided robust questioning of witnesses. For the inquiry to retain—or, more accurately, obtain—public confidence, raising issues will not suffice; the most rigorous cross-examination of contentious points must be pursued. And that is the stock-in-trade of barristers.

The substantive question is the rather more nebulous issue of international law, and the rights and wrongs of the Iraq war thereunder.

The international law question has already been authoritatively discussed by Professor Greer and Dr Tsagourias (NLJ 2010, vol 160, p 475). I would respectfully suggest that the comparison in their last paragraph between Iraq and Kosovo is the key point, and in fact renders much of the public debate on Iraq (and indeed the Chilcott Inquiry itself) misplaced. The reason that Iraq remains in the public eye is not that there were no weapons of mass destruction (WMD), nor because there is doubt over the Prime Minister's intentions, nor that the war was of doubtful international legality. It is because—

Published in the *New Law Journal*, vol 160, 7 May 2010, p 634.

and almost only because—the aftermath of the invasion was a fiasco.

It is worth remembering that the initial invasion in 2003 was an almost unprecedented military success. The coalition achieved its stated objective of deposing the Iraqi regime in a few short weeks, with minimal casualties. The problem is that that seems to have been about as far as the pre-invasion planning ever got. The infrastructure of the country was largely destroyed or disbanded and there was accordingly little to check—and everything to encourage—the insurgency that followed.

The occupying troops were too few in number, primarily trained to fight a conventional war rather than counter-insurgency, and constrained by rules of engagement that most certainly were not going to be observed in reciprocation by the insurgents. Readers will need no reminding of the blood that was shed thereafter, and even if some significant progress has been made since the US "surge", the cost in money and lives has been severe and even the most optimistic commentators have ceased to speak in terms of ultimate victory. That is why the public continues to demand investigation and indeed recrimination, and every aspect of the political, military, constitutional and legal steps to war remain under scrutiny.

Suppose, however, that, by whatever means, Iraq had been transformed almost seamlessly after the invasion into a functioning democracy with a low crime rate, no insurgency to speak of and tangible respect for human rights. The politicians responsible would now be feted as great statesmen and women, and there is no chance whatsoever that seven years later there would be any inquiry poring over the finer nuances of international law, the Attorney General's advice, and precisely who knew what and when regarding WMD.

The point can reiterated by returning to the Kosovo war of 1999. Public debate regarding that war ceased fairly shortly after the conclusion of combat operations. And yet, contrary to the statements by the executive at the time, there seems little doubt that the war was indeed illegal. The United Nations Charter authorises military action only with a Security Council resolution or where it is conducted in self-defence.

No prior Security Council resolution was ever obtained for the NATO intervention. NATO could not claim to be acting in self defence. Yugoslavia's complaint at the International Court of Justice in April 1999, filed against ten NATO members, foundered on the basis that Yugoslavia was not a member of the UN during the war. In 2000, however, the House of Commons Select Committee on Foreign Affairs found that the war was illegal, though it offered by way of mitigation the conclusion that: "NATO's military action, if of dubious legality in the current state of international law, was justified on moral grounds."

The morality of the Kosovo war probably remains a moot point, but it would certainly not be if the outcome of NATO's actions had been bloodshed on the same scale as Iraq. The consensus in that case would be that the disaster was foreseeable all along and that the UK government had acted recklessly. Arguments about Serbian atrocities would have cut no ice: Milosovic's crimes, though serious, were not in the same league as those of Saddam Hussein, and the removal of Saddam Hussein is no longer seen as a justification for Operation Telic.

It follows that the Chilcott Inquiry should be concentrating almost all of its energies on the precise steps that were taken to plan for the aftermath of the removal of the Iraqi regime. It is unlikely that those responsible for the post-invasion planning will be held to account, legally or otherwise. More is the pity, for it is they who have the most to answer for.

16. Nothing to see here: the Libyan intervention

Imagine that a Predator drone, controlled by a foreign state, circles above the White House looking for President Obama. It fires a missile but misses the President and kills a couple of innocent civilians instead. The foreign state then issues a statement saying it is sorry about the civilians but Obama's position is untenable and the drones will keep coming until he leaves office.

It is not difficult to imagine the response from the White House. President Obama would make a speech in short order evoking the stirring rhetoric of President Roosevelt's post-Pearl Harbor address, or President Bush's on 9/11, and the television news would soon be flooded with images of American forces setting off to unleash retribution.

Suppose further that the responsible state was not acting alone, but was receiving technical, material and intelligence assistance from another state. If so, that state would also find itself on the Pentagon's target list.

The ensuing clash of arms might be called many things, but no-one could argue that it would appropriately be called a "war".

I make that rather laboured point because of the startling position the White House took on Libya. In a detailed document prepared in June 2011, the White House asserted that because the US forces involved were only playing a "supporting role", they were not engaged in "hostilities".

Accordingly, the argument ran, the definition of "hostilities" as described under the War Powers Resolution of 1973 had not been met. That resolution, part of the fallout over the Vietnam War, requires Congressional approval for any deployment of US forces in hostilities for

Published on both *Halsbury's Law Exchange* and *Legalweek.com* on 22 August 2011.

more than 60 days. The White House said that its forces in Libya are not engaged in sustained fighting or "active exchanges of fire with hostile forces".

With the caveat that I am not an American lawyer, that argument seems entirely fallacious. The governments responsible for the intervention made clear early on that Gaddafi's regime could not continue.

NATO's operations began after UN Resolution 1973, which was passed when it was thought a slaughter of citizens by Gaddafi's troops was imminent, the sanctions and other measures brought in by Resolution 1970 having failed to prevent the civil war. Initially the intention was to establish a no-fly zone, then to use "all necessary measures" to defend civilians. In turn the coalition took it to mean that Gaddafi's regime had to be removed.

We therefore went from attempting to prevent a massacre in a particular time and place to attempting to overthrow a sovereign government by the use of military force. The latter in anyone's language is a war. The fact that our involvement has been limited to naval blockading and acting as the rebels' air force is not relevant: we have been deploying armed forces in active operations. Rumour has it that we or our coalition partners have supplied weapons to the rebels as well and it seems a shade implausible that there have been no special forces operations in the area.

The only distinction that the White House offered was that there was no danger to American servicemen. That was a matter of good fortune for them, but to suggest that their operations were not thereby a "war" strains logic beyond breaking point. As I tried to show above, it is an argument that would cut no ice in the other direction.

We have therefore been, *pace* President Obama, at war with the sovereign government of Libya. A number of serious questions then arise. For a start, even if the war is legal, what is the legal imperative for the UK's involvement? What of all the other states who supported the resolution?

The second question concerns the moral justification. If on the balance of probabilities military intervention would save more lives than it would cost then it might well be justified. That is difficult to judge, to put it mildly.

It is true that the fact that we are selective in our use of force by not intervening in, say, Syria, is not an argument against intervening in Libya: if I fail to save ten drowning people it would still be morally correct to save the eleventh, even though I am being inconsistent by doing so.

Apparently we intervened to stop a massacre of civilians by Gaddafi's forces in Benghazi. Apparently we succeeded. But it also seems that we have little clue as to what happens next. There was no doubt a hope that Gaddafi would flee once Western air power was deployed against him. That faded quickly, and should have been to no-one's surprise: air power tends not to do that.

However, it now seems that Gaddafi is indeed about to fall.* What then are our obligations in international law, having toppled him? What plan is in place for a substitute government? What if an Iraqi-style internecine civil war erupts? I have yet to read reassuring answers to any of those questions.

One can easily understand why our leaders support the notion of "liberal intervention". It is their best chance of being remembered as statesmen rather than jobbing politicians. It is no doubt more professionally rewarding flying to Washington on a private jet and making speeches at the White House than trying to deal with more mundane matters such as the NHS budget, another banking failure or a school closure in the provinces. But the executive should also consider that if international law is fraught with uncertainty, military action is too, and inevitably risks the most severe consequences in terms of blood and treasure. And if there is one lesson from Iraq, it is that removing dictators is only the very beginning of what might be a long and difficult story. Perhaps there will be a smooth transition from Gaddafi to a democratic government supporting human rights and the rule of law. Or perhaps there won't be.

* Gaddafi was captured and killed on 20 October 2011.

17. A modern-day "conchie"

Introduction

Conscientious objection to military service has provided much drama in both fiction and real life for many years. In fiction one finds examples in the recent *Downton Abbey*, or the gentle Private Godfrey in *Dad's Army* and countless other works as well.

The most famous non-fiction example is possibly Mohammed Ali, who chose jail and the suspension of his boxing career rather than serving in Vietnam against an enemy he did not know on behalf of a state that declined to afford him full civil rights.

Recently in this country the case of *R v Lyons* [2011] EWCA Crim 2808 raised the same issue in the context of Britain's modern wars.

Lyons joined the Royal Navy and rose to the rank of leading medical assistant. In May 2010 he was told he would be deployed to Afghanistan. He formed the view that the UK's involvement in the conflict was wrong and that it would be morally wrong for him to take part. He therefore applied for discharge from the Navy on the ground that he was a conscientious objector. The application was refused and he appealed. Before his appeal was determined, he was ordered to undertake a pre-deployment weapons training course. He refused to participate. He was court-martialled and found guilty of intentionally disobeying a lawful command contrary to s 12(1)(a) of the Armed Forces Act 2006. He was sentenced to seven months' military detention, demoted to able seaman and dismissed from the service. He appealed against sentence.

Published in *Criminal Law & Justice Weekly*, vol 176, 3 March 2012, p 135. With thanks to Guy Skelton for his assistance.

Historical background

Objection to war – be it a particular conflict or warfare in general – on the grounds of religion, secular morality or simple emotion is no doubt as old as war itself. In Britain it has been less of an issue since the armed forces have historically been recruited on a volunteer basis. Full-scale conscription was in fact unknown in this country until the Great War, when the British Army found itself drawn irrevocably into the sort of full-scale conflict on the Continent which it had spent a century planning to avoid. By contrast, most continental powers had had compulsory military service for generations, the modern origins lying in the French Revolution and the subsequent creation of the Grande Armée.

It is therefore interesting to note that Britain was the first amongst European powers to have formal legal recognition of conscientious objection. Mention was made in the Militia Act 1757, but the story in modern times begins with the Military Service Act 1916, an Act which simultaneously introduced conscription and the recognition of objection on the ground of conscience.

During the Second World War, nearly 60,000 registered as conscientious objectors. After national service ended at the start of the 1960s, formal procedures for dealing with conscientious objectors fell away, until in 1970 the Advisory Committee on Conscientious Objectors (ACCO) was formed as a non-departmental public body to advise the Secretary of State for Defence.

The law

The procedure in force at the time of Lyons' case (it has since been altered) was set out in Personnel, Legal, Administrative and General Orders 0801 (PLAGO 0801). PLAGOs were orders made under the executive power of the Crown and dealt with matters of naval personnel management. Paragraph 1 of PLAGO 0801 provided:

> "Any RN/RM officer or rating/other rank who claims to have developed a genuine conscientious objection to further service may apply for premature discharge

without regard to length of service or the manpower situation in the branch ... "

Lyons' case

Lyons' primary submission was that his claim to be a conscientious objector was protected by his right to freedom of religion under Art 9 of the European Convention on Human Rights. Secondly, he contended that the order for medical staff to undergo weapons training had been contrary to the Geneva Convention. Thirdly, he contended that he had a valid defence under s 12 of the 2006 Act if he believed the order to be unlawful, as he would thereby lack the requisite *mens rea*. Finally, he appealed against sentence on the ground that it was manifestly excessive.

With respect to Art 9, Lyons' case was that it required that from the moment when a member of the armed forces told his commanding officer that he objected to further service on the ground of conscientious objection, he could not be required to take any part in active service until his claim had been finally determined. Alternatively he contended that his right to refuse would begin at the moment when he made a written application for discharge. He referred to *Bayatan v Armenia* [2011] ECHR 23459/03, in which the European Court of Human Rights (ECtHR) departed from previous authority and held that Art 9 could support a claim for conscientious objection.

Both submissions failed. There would be obvious and potentially grave consequences for military operations, the safety of other members of the forces and possibly civilian populations as well. It would mean that one or more members of a unit in a dangerous situation could suddenly refuse to take any further part in the operation on which they had been deployed, which would entail all manner of risk.

The court concluded that:

"A person who voluntarily enters military service undertakes serious responsibilities potentially involving the lives and safety of others. If he seeks to be discharged from further service on the ground of conscientious objection, it is right that there should be a proper process for deciding whether his claim is well-founded. Until that has been established it is necessary and just that he should continue to be subject to the requirements of military service and military discipline ..."

As to the Geneva Convention, the court began with the observation that the Taliban did not seem bothered about complying with it, having fired on medical personnel in the past. But either way there was no basis for contending that the policy of training medical personnel in weapons prior to service was in any way unlawful.

The *mens rea* argument was dismissed in an equally summary fashion: there was nothing in the wording of s 12 of the 2006 Act justifying the submission and it would seriously undermine the purpose of the Act if one was to read in an extra requirement that the person knew or believed the command to be a lawful command.

Finally the court dismissed the appeal against sentence: the board had been in a far better position to assess the effect of Lyons' conduct.

Discussion

The result of the case was inevitable on the law. No detailed military knowledge is required to envisage the chaos that could ensue from anyone being rendered exempt from service from the moment they claimed to be a conscientious objector, or even from the moment they set down such a claim in writing. That would apply whether in peacetime or in war, though obviously the latter would carry more immediate and serious consequences. Even in peacetime the armed forces are supposed to maintain a high degree of readiness, which in turn requires risky and complex training exercises, all of which would have been jeopardised had Lyons' argument been accepted.

Two issues remain. First, conscientious objection has traditionally been associated with religious belief, and in Lyons' case his chaplain concluded that he was not a conscientious objector but rather someone "who had a political objection to a particular military engagement." Yet the distinction is unjustifiable. Why should an objection on religious grounds be stronger than, say, Mohammed Ali's?

The ECtHR in *Bayatan* seemed to agree when referring to opposition to service on the ground of "deeply and genuinely held religious *or other* beliefs ..." (emphasis added).

The decision of the Employment Appeal Tribunal in *Nicholson v Grainger plc* [2009] All ER (D) 59 (Nov) provides a good example of the knots the courts can tie themselves into when trying to equate a philosophical or political belief with a religious one. The tribunal in that case fashioned a tortuous test to determine which non-religious beliefs had the same status as religion: (i) the belief had to be genuinely held; (ii) it had to be a belief and not an opinion or viewpoint based on the present state of information available; (iii) it had to be a belief as to a weighty and substantial aspect of human life and behaviour; (iv) it had to attain a certain level of cogency, seriousness, cohesion and importance; and (v) it had to be worthy of respect in a democratic society, be not incompatible with human dignity and not conflict with the fundamental rights of others.

I doubt whether the test is workable: the courts are ill-suited to making Olympian judgments on a man or woman's soul and the state should not be deciding what beliefs are worthy of respect in the first place.

Secondly, and finally, there is the most fundamental question of all, taken for granted in Lyons' case – whether there is any justification for conscientious objection in the first place. There is no lawful recognition of conscientious objection to taxation despite many people having beliefs against it that would have as good a chance as any of passing the *Nicholson v Grainger* test. The counter-argument is that all benefit from taxation and therefore all must pay it. Logically the same might be said for defence – the more so with an all-volunteer army.

Of course a man can join up and then change his mind, as Lyons apparently did; but the answer then is to resign in accordance with the contract, not try to circumvent it.

Part IV: Personal Battles

The cases in this part have little in common other than the fact that they were brought by an individual litigant, as opposed to a multi-national corporation or some other faceless entity. I rather enjoy the fact that they show a human side to the legal process: be they concerned citizens, disgruntled celebrities or wine critics, each case involves an individual who felt wronged and looked to the law courts for redress, though not all got what they wished for.

Each also involved some fundamental principles of law: freedom of speech, the right to privacy, children's rights, Aboriginal land rights and the most fundamental of all, the right to life.

Irony abounds in many of the stories. Mrs Gillick's name became synonymous with children's rights – the very thing she wanted to stop. It rather reminded me of Mary Whitehouse, an earlier crusader against changing public morals. Mrs Whitehouse wrote to the screenwriter Johnny Speight complaining about his programme *Til Death Us Do Part*; the very next episode had Alf Garnett reading out some of her pamphlets and strongly agreeing with all of them. Mrs Gillick for her part went to court to stop one thing (contraception advice to teenagers without parental knowledge or consent) and ended up substantially creating another (the modern concept of children's rights).

Eddie Mabo achieved legal immortality in Australia but his iron will – such an asset in his court battles – seems to have rendered him rather unpopular in his personal life although it made him a hero after his death.

There is no humour in the cases of Diane Pretty and Debbie Purdy. Unquestionably the greatest tragedy was that of Ms Pretty. She fought a legal battle to try and avoid an agonising death from her condition. She lost the case and later suffered the very death she had feared. Since Debbie Purdy's subsequent case, guidelines have been formulated on prosecuting assisted suicide, but it remains, inevitably, the most emotive of all legal and moral disputes.

Next there is the case which, I have to say, infuriated me more than any other in this book – the libel action brought by the British Chiropractic Association against the writer Simon Singh. One can only express gratitude for the service to the nation Dr Singh performed by resisting what amounted to a disgraceful piece of bullying and a gross affront to freedom of speech. Hopefully the Association, and those of its ilk, have learned their lesson.

More on free speech follows, with an equally dismal case from Hungary, where a wine critic was subject to criminal libel proceedings for being rude about a wine. The fact that it is the job of a wine critic to be rude about wines he or she does not like did not seem to bother the Hungarian courts. The fact that the criminal law should only be used against criminals rather than irascible authors did not trouble them either.

18. Negative returns

On my first day as an aspiring litigator, a partner gave some advice: litigation always goes wrong. Perhaps there was some exaggeration, but it was a sound enough warning. After all, at least half of all litigants would probably agree.

Most often the negative consequences of losing a case are simply financial, but for others rather worse may come of it. Oscar Wilde sued the Marquess of Queensberry; not only did he lose, but he received a criminal prosecution for his trouble. A more tolerant age did not help Lord Browne of Madingley, who wanted to keep details of his former relationship quiet. He started by insisting that deference be paid to his status as the senior businessman in the land and a peer of the realm – in contradistinction, he argued, to the lowly status of his erstwhile partner and the Sunday papers who wished to publish the story. He finished by being exposed as a liar and losing his business positions into the bargain, all for the sake of the most trivial and irrelevant personal details. Jonathan Aitken, meanwhile, fell on his own sword (of truth ...).

Perhaps, however, the most ironically self-destructive consequence of a failed case is when the unsuccessful litigant's name becomes immortalised as legal shorthand for the very thing he or she tried to prevent. One unfortunate Mr Scott, in the midst of the prudish Edwardian age, took exception to his wife highlighting his marital inadequacies, and sought to have any such evidence heard in private. The point was ultimately decided by the House of Lords against him, in what remains the leading authority on open justice today (*Scott v Scott* [1911-13] All ER Rep 1).

Suffering a similar fate in more recent times was Mrs Victoria Gillick. In 1980, the then Department of

Published in the *New Law Journal*, vol 161, 4 February 2011, p 178.

Health and Social Security issued a policy which would have enabled children under the age of 16 to receive contraceptive advice and treatment without their parents' knowledge, much less permission. Mrs Gillick, the mother of ten children including five daughters, was not having that. She brought proceedings seeking a declaration that the policy was unlawful. Famously, her case failed before the House of Lords. She was then left with having established a new principle regarding the circumstances in which children might consent to treatment without parental permission, known to the present day as "Gillick-competence".

As with many other legal tales it could all have turned out rather differently. The law lords' decision was given by a majority of one. They held that while it would be unusual for a doctor to give the advice to a child under 16 without the consent of her parents, the parents' right to decide effectively ended once the child had achieved sufficient understanding and intelligence to understand fully what was proposed.

That was a significant development from the previous doctrine, under which the concept of parental rights and control had ruled the roost.

Almost immediately the question arose as to whether the child's right to accept treatment also carried with it the right to refuse treatment; the Court of Appeal in subsequent cases did not think so. It remains an interesting moral conundrum: should a child competent to understand treatment be dragged into an operating theatre against her wishes? A similar logical point arises with assisted suicide: if a person has the right to refuse to take a drug even if the consequences will be almost immediately fatal, do they also have the right to accept "treatment" in the form of a fatal drug?

The lasting significance of Gillick has been the shift from parental rights to the overarching principle of the "best interests of the child". That was reflected in the Children Act 1989 and the accompanying Family Proceedings Rules 1991. One practical consequence has been the increased opportunity for children to participate in legal proceedings. In general it may now be said that once a child has developed a certain level of intelligence and maturity, the parents' decision-making rights fall away, or at least are greatly diminished (see Janet Bazley QC and Stephen Jarmain "Gillick and the dwindling right of parental authority" in *Cases that Changed Our Lives*, LexisNexis 2010).

Mrs Gillick would not have been amused. Today she might be considered somewhat old fashioned, certainly in her view of sexual morality. Opinion columns confirm that the merits of that change in public morals remain as disputed as ever.

But Mrs Gillick was also old fashioned in another respect: she held principles that went beyond her immediate personal gratification, and was prepared to stand up when she saw public injustice. Perhaps most readers might bemoan the diminishing of that ethos, even if we may differ from Mrs Gillick over what in fact constitutes public injustice.

Afterword

Mrs Gillick was not done with the legal system. She returned to sue the BBC and a journalist, Susan Pearce, for libel following comments about the effect of her victory in the Court of Appeal. She won a preliminary ruling before the Court of Appeal ((1995) *Times*, 20 October), but ultimately the case was thrown out before it reached the jury. She was left penniless, but told the *Guardian* newspaper she intended to carry on with her public campaigns nevertheless (see *Guardian*, 21 November 2000):

> "They say that only dead fish swim with the tide. I don't want to be one of those dead bloaters."

Not many could accuse her of that.

19. Revenge of the Mer-man

Prime Minister David Cameron recently attracted a few headlines when, referring to the standoff between India and Pakistan over Kashmir, he suggested that "with so many of the problems of the world, we are responsible for their creation in the first place". Needless to say, opinion was divided, both on the accuracy of his statement and the merits of him saying it whether true or not.

One thing Britain certainly did create, in 1788, was the modern state of Australia. At the time, it was considered that there were three ways in which title to land could be acquired: conquest, cession, and *terra nullius* – land with no human occupants. An inconvenience obviously arose for the last of those concepts if the land was bigger than first thought and it turned out that there were, after all, some people already living there. In response, a most offensive gloss was added by European lawyers to the effect that "primitive tribes" did not count, as they had no recognisable legal system. The Australian Aborigines found themselves labelled as such.

Lumped in with the same fate were the inhabitants of the tiny Murray Islands, three islands with a combined area of just nine square miles, situated in the Torres Strait (the sea between Australia and Papua New Guinea). The islanders were descendants of the Meriam people, whose ancestry long pre-dated European settlements in the South Pacific. As the Australian colony grew, the colonial office in London and the fledgling local administration decided to extend the boundaries, and to that end the Murray Islands were declared annexed to the colony of Queensland in 1879.

The problem was that no one had taken the trouble to tell the locals about the annexation before the event. Just over half a century later, in 1936, one Eddie Mabo was born on Mer, the largest of the islands. His was not an

Published in the *New Law Journal*, vol 161, 29 April 2011, p 602.

easy start in life. His mother died while he was in infancy. As a teenager he was exiled by the strict island council for a prank. He worked a few jobs before a stint as a gardener at James Cook University in Townsville. There he took exception to a conversation about ownership of land on the islands: as far as he was concerned his people, never having agreed otherwise, remained the rightful owners.

In 1981, Mabo addressed a conference at the University about the inheritance system on the islands, and thereafter a decade of litigation in his name began to determine the question of the ownership of the land. It was finally concluded in mid-1992 by the High Court of Australia (*Mabo v State of Queensland (No 2)* (1992) 175 CLR 1). The court declared that there was a system of native title (namely, interests and rights of indigenous inhabitants in land, under traditional laws and customs) recognised by the Islanders in 1879, which had not automatically been extinguished by the exercise of sovereignty by the Australian government (subject to certain exceptions). It was further declared that the traditional title had not been extinguished by subsequent legislation or executive act and could not be extinguished without the payment of compensation to the traditional titleholders. Further, the land was not Crown land within the meaning of the relevant Australian statute.

The effect of the ruling was emphatically to pour the doctrine of terra nullius with regard to the islands back into its bottle.

Not unusually for a cause célèbre, much of the reaction in the popular press combined hysteria with inaccuracy, but as things transpired, the decision led neither to the extinction of private property rights as feared by some, nor to ultimate satisfaction of all Aboriginal claims as hoped by others. Subsequent cases fleshed out the caveats in the original judgment, including conditions for the establishment of native title and a reiteration that native title extinguished by a sovereign power could not later be revived, because thereafter only the sovereign power could create title.

Many Aboriginal claims have since been settled rather than proceeding through the courts, though the conduct of the negotiations would have been against the backdrop of the *Mabo* ruling. The importance of the case and the resultant vindication of Eddie Mabo's actions remain unquestioned (see Dr Kevin Lindgren QC, "Native Title in Australia" in *Cases That Changed Our Lives*, LexisNexis, 2010).

For Eddie Mabo himself, however, tragedy seemed to be present as much as triumph. He was denied permission by his own community to return to his dying father, on the basis that he was a trouble maker ... Then, with even crueller irony, he contracted cancer and died five months before the High Court gave the judgment for which his name will always remain legal shorthand.

So much for *das Pathetisch-Erhabene*. The native title doctrine has no relevance in England, but that does not mean Eddie Mabo's story should not be of interest to English lawyers. It was rather fatuous of Mr Cameron to lump the blame for present day Kashmir on the British: the governments of India and Pakistan are large and sophisticated entities who should not be excused blame for a situation that has been in their hands for decades.

By contrast, Eddie Mabo and his people, as we have seen, had their land taken by a decree of which they were not even told, and were not in the position of a sovereign state to do anything about it. A century of presumption by those who governed Australia did not alter the (im)morality of the situation. By 1992, of course, responsibility had long passed from Britain to the independent state of Australia, who at last set about righting the historical wrong.

20. Unmitigated tragedy: Diane Pretty and Debbie Purdy

For the most obvious of reasons, assisted suicide constitutes one of the most emotive of all legal issues. It is no great surprise then that the issue still receives regular press attention and continues to evoke the strongest of opposing viewpoints.

On 3 September 2010, two people were arrested in relation to the suicide of a severely disabled 76-year-old retired pensioner, Donald Sinclair, who suffered from a motor neurone disease. Mr Sinclair had travelled to Switzerland in order to die at Dignitas, a clinic for voluntary euthanasia.

The story recalled two of the most famous recent cases in English law, those of the terminally ill Diane Pretty and Debbie Purdy. Both suffered conditions similar to that of Mr Sinclair, and each brought legal proceedings because they wished to die in circumstances of their own choosing.

There are two formidable issues with which law makers in this area have to deal. The first is whether or not assisted suicide should be permitted at all. The second (assuming one believes it should be) is how to create a workable legal framework to allow it.

As to the first issue, a full consideration would easily fill many books, involving as it does competing moral, cultural and religious viewpoints. Some believe suicide is wrong whether assisted or unassisted. Even those in favour would concede the risk that an apparently voluntary assisted suicide might transpire to have been brought about by improper pressure. Others consider it an issue of personal autonomy, and that everyone has a right to end their lives in the circumstances of their own choosing. Then there is a logical point: it is generally accepted (and certainly is the law) that an adult of full

Published in *Criminal Law & Justice Weekly*, vol 174, 6 November 2010, p 695. Co-written with Lynne Townley.

mental capacity has the unfettered right to refuse medical treatment of any sort – even if they will die in very short order without it. If one has the right to refuse treatment despite the fact that certain death will follow almost immediately, then arguably it follows that they should also have the right to accept treatment with the same result.

One then turns to the second issue of devising a legal framework to permit assisted suicide. The Pretty and Purdy cases (see [2002] 1 All ER 1 and [2009] 4 All ER 1147 respectively) examined the English legal situation in close detail. The key point is that although it remains an offence under s 2(1) of the Suicide Act 1961 to assist or encourage the suicide of another (see also the amendment provided by s 2A, introduced in January 2010), it is a fundamental rule under English law that prosecutorial authorities have a discretion whether or not to bring a prosecution in any individual case, even when it seems clear that an offence has been committed; and in fact the prosecutors in England and Wales have exercised that discretion in some cases not to prosecute under s 2(1).

Following an extensive consultation procedure after Debbie Purdy's case, the Crown Prosecution Service (CPS) issued guidelines in February 2010 on how that discretion would be exercised. Factors in favour of a prosecution include where the victim was under 18, or lacked the capacity to reach an informed decision, and where the suspect was not wholly motivated by compassion. Factors tending against prosecution include where the victim had reached a voluntary, clear, settled and informed decision, and the suspect was motivated wholly by compassion.

Inevitably, however, whilst those guidelines make the law much clearer, they have done nothing to foreclose the moral debate. The author Sir Terry Pratchett, who suffers from Alzheimer's disease, has spoken in favour of a tribunal comprising suitably qualified people, which would assess anyone seeking an assisted death and judge whether they were in fact acting of their own volition with full mental capacity.

The prospect of such "death tribunals" can hardly be uncontroversial, but unless the terminally ill can obtain prior approval they will be left with the fear that caused Debbie Purdy such distress: namely that their closest relatives might be prosecuted after the event. In those circumstances they may choose to end their own lives whilst they still retain the physical ability to do so – or they may wait and suffer the agonizing death that Diane Pretty endured because she did not receive the legal approbation which she sought.

It may therefore be that a tribunal is the least-worst option, but even its adoption would hardly end the practical difficulties. Would representation before the tribunal be publicly funded? Who else would be entitled to make representations? Would the tribunal's decisions be judicially reviewable? How long would the decision-making process take (this would be particularly important in the case of sufferers of degenerative illnesses)?

An independent legal think-tank, Halsbury's Law Exchange, is presently compiling a White Paper on assisted suicide, and no doubt it will result in a much fuller discussion of the subject than has been possible here. It will not be short of material.*

* The Paper, written by Jon Cooper QC and published in January 2012, was indeed not short of material. Mr Cooper concluded that the existing guidelines went further than the House of Lords had intended in Ms Purdy's case, but that they could be made to work when read in light of the existing body of case law on the issue. At about the same time, a report by Lord Falconer QC argued strongly for legalisation of assisted suicide, and provoked the inevitably strong reactions throughout the press and elsewhere.

21. Sticks and stones

"Sticks and stones may break my bones", went a popular refrain of my primary school days, "but names will never harm me".

Made of somewhat less sturdy material is the British Chiropractic Association (the Association), which took exception to an article by the scientist and author Dr Simon Singh in the *Guardian* newspaper. Its response is an object lesson in why free speech needs robust defending, as indeed does the teaching of science and the scientific method.

The *Guardian* article to which the Association objected included the following:

> "The British Chiropractic Association claims that their members can help treat children with colic, sleeping and feeding problems, frequent ear infections, asthma and prolonged crying, even though there is not a jot of evidence. This organisation is the respectable face of the chiropractic profession and yet it happily promotes bogus treatments."

Ignoring the journalistic context, this is the ordinary stuff of scientific debate: the Association made certain claims for which Dr Singh disputed the evidence. The appropriate response for the Association would have been to adduce peer-reviewed evidence supporting its claims and for those to be subjected to further study and testing. Over time either or both sides should then have modified or abandoned their views depending on the weight of the evidence. Any number of fora existed for the Association to propound its viewpoint: indeed, the *Guardian* itself offered just such an opportunity by inviting them to write a response to Dr Singh of the same length and which would have been given the same degree of prominence in the newspaper.

But the Association did not take that course. Instead it chose to sue for libel. Not the obvious defendant of the *Guardian* newspaper, but Dr Singh personally.

It takes little imagination to work out why. The *Guardian* would have been well placed to defend any such action. But Dr Singh was a private individual and, though reasonably well-off, hardly in the position of a national newspaper to afford the cost of High Court litigation. It is not unreasonable to assume that the Association hoped not only to silence Dr Singh, but also to send a message to anyone else who dared cross them in the same fashion.

The Court of Appeal had this to say of that tawdry strategy:

> "It is now nearly two years since the publication of the offending article. It seems unlikely that anyone would dare repeat the opinions expressed by Dr Singh for fear of a writ. Accordingly this litigation has almost certainly had a chilling effect on public debate which might otherwise have assisted potential patients to make informed choices about the possible use of chiropractic. If so, quite apart from any public interest in issues of legal principle which arise in the present proceedings, the questions raised by Dr Singh, which have a direct resonance for patients, are unresolved. This would be a surprising consequence of laws designed to protect reputation ... "

Fortunately it was not the ultimate consequence of the litigation. Dr Singh found the resources not only to defend the action in the High Court, but to appeal successfully against an adverse finding that his article could not amount to "fair comment".

The evidence proffered by the Association is revealing in itself. The Court of Appeal quoted the following:

> "The BCA ... relies (among other studies) on a 1989 observational study of 316 children, of which it is said:
>
> 'This .... measured the number of hours each child spent in crying. It showed a reduction in crying time from 5.2 hours each day to 0.65 hours each day at 14 days. This was a very substantial improvement. There was no control group. However, the study constitutes evidence.'"

It is, however, elementary medical science that the only evidence worthy of the name comes from double blind, randomised control tests. The Association's quoted "observational study" admits that it had no control group. To suggest it constitutes evidence is a classic example of the *post hoc ergo propter hoc* fallacy. It is difficult to rebut the suspicion that the lack of scientific validity of this "observational study" might be the reason why the Association opted for a libel suit rather than the proper course of a public debate about the evidence for its claims.

The Court of Appeal also quoted the following pithy observation from an American judgment (*Underwager v Salter* 22 Fed. 3d 730 (1994)):

> "[Plaintiffs] cannot, by simply filing suit and crying 'character assassination!', silence those who hold divergent views, no matter how adverse those views may be to plaintiffs' interests. Scientific controversies must be settled by the methods of science rather than by the methods of litigation. ... More papers, more discussion, better data, and more satisfactory models – not larger awards of damages – mark the path towards superior understanding of the world around us."

With which it is impossible to disagree. The nub of the story is that libel laws should have nothing to do with scientific debate.

The irony is that by adopting its bullying tactics and failing, the Association ultimately did itself more damage – both financially and in terms of its reputation – than Dr Singh's original article ever would have done if it had been simply ignored. It richly deserved that fate.

22. A non-vintage case

In 1976, the famous "Paris Tasting" took place in the French capital. Organised by an Englishman, Steven Spurrier, a selection of judges drawn from the *haute société* of French wine undertook a blind tasting and found, to their amazement, that they preferred unknown Californian wine to some classic French offerings. The event amounted to a watershed in the history of non-French wine: more than three decades on, the shelves of wine merchants now heave with offerings from across the globe. As well as the New World, the event also benefited older regions, with the realisation that perhaps France did not have a monopoly on the best terroir after all.

One such older region was Hungary, whose tradition of wine making dates back to Roman times. In fact, Magyar has the distinction of being the only language apart from Greek which has a name for wine that is not derived from Latin. Hungary is best known for a dessert wine, Tokaji, and the arrestingly named red wine Egri Bikavér, or "Bull's Blood of Eger."

By 2011 Hungary had ostensibly shaken off Communism for two decades, meaning that its wine merchants had had ample time to find new export markets. But the case of *Uj v Hungary* (App. No. 23954/10, 19 July 2011) before the European Court of Human Rights (ECtHR), concerning a particular variety of Hungarian wine, shows that they had not entirely exorcised the Soviet ghost by that time. The case provides some justification for the oft-maligned institution of the Strasbourg Court, and reminds us in England that we ought to be more appreciative of our own tradition of free speech.

The applicant, one Mr Uj, was a journalist. In 2008 he published an article in the opinion column of a national daily newspaper. The subject was a well-known Hungarian wine variety produced by a state-owned

Published in the *New Law Journal* , vol 162, 17 August 2012, p 1094.

corporation, T Zrt Mr Uj was at a loss to understand the wine's popularity. He explained that the wine was "shit", opined that it was a national embarrassment and rubbished T Zrt for making it.

T Zrt's response was not to take Mr Uj's jabs on the chin, but to bring a law suit. Not simply a civil claim either, but a "criminal complaint" which led to a conviction of ragalmazas, or defamation. The court held that the article went beyond the boundaries of journalistic opinion and "amounted to stating a fact susceptible of harming the reputation of the producer of the wine variety in question". It imposed a penalty which seems to have been akin to a suspended sentence.

Mr Uj appealed. The appellate court held that he should have a criminal conviction, but the sentence should be reduced to a "reprimand". Its reasoning was that although he had been entitled to express his opinion, he had overstepped the mark by saying "shit", much like the Sex Pistols (the court did not add) on television in the year of the Paris tasting.

Mr Uj's further appeal to the Hungarian Supreme Court was dismissed. He then applied to the ECtHR, contending that his right to free speech under Art 10 of the European Convention on Human Rights had been breached.

There was no dispute that there had been an interference with Art 10. The government argued, however, that the expression was "so offensive that the ... prosecution had corresponded to a pressing social need" and that, since Mr Uj had only ended up with a reprimand, the interference could not be considered disproportionate.

The ECtHR swiftly dismantled that argument. The article was not a defamatory statement of fact but a value judgment or opinion. It constituted a satirical denouncement of the company within the context of state economic policies and consumer attitudes. The vulgarity of the particular epithet might be regretted but it was a common one in the context of low-quality wine.

The interference with Art 10 had not been justified and therefore Mr Uj's right had been violated.

From an English perspective the mere fact of the proceedings, never mind the conviction, bordered on the astonishing. Ignoring the prose, which one cannot judge in translation, the content of the article would be familiar to any readers of English papers. It seems almost a requirement of restaurant hacks in this country to be as rude as possible, and many use language at least as salty as that of Mr Uj.

The English hacks might be said to be following a tradition of satire that dates back to Swift and Hogarth, and a tradition of criticism that is much older than that. In short, no-one in England would have blinked an eye at what was written and any attempt at criminal proceedings would – or should – have been laughed out of court, though I should add that our libel laws have occasionally gone off the rails in recent years.

Astonishment aside, the case gives some pause for thought. Economists would note disapprovingly that the hand of the state was still meddling in the wine market in Hungary. Worse, the same hand was still clapping itself over the mouths of journalists in a manner disturbingly redolent of Hungary's Communist past. In England the press regularly denounces the ECtHR. In Hungary, on the other hand, one expects that Mr Uj and his journalist colleagues would be very grateful for it indeed.

Part V: Religion and the Law

Religion and the law has become a much more common form of dispute in the United Kingdom in the twenty-first century than it was for most of the twentieth. When I first came across the issue at university in New Zealand in the early 1990s, I was puzzled that it could even arise in a Western country at that time. After some searching I wondered if there might be a question about religious parents wanting to home-school their children, or preclude them from having blood transfusions, but that was about it.

Of course there were more issues than that, but nothing like the number of high-profile cases that made legal headlines in Britain in 2010 and 2011 as the courts sought to balance the competing rights of religious minorities with other rights such as equality of gender and sexual orientation, within the framework (or battlefield) of the Human Rights Act 1998.

Although the different considerations are many, it seems to me that the essence of most disputes over religion and the law can be stated simply. As a starting point, everyone has the right to practise his or her religion. Everyone also has the right to do as they please with their own premises. Employers may choose whomsoever they wish for their staff. At the same time, everyone has the right not to be discriminated against on the basis of race, religion, gender or sexual orientation.

The question is how to balance those different rights when they clash. If a religious employer wants all members of her or his staff to be practising members of the religion, one might say that no outsider has the right to object. But does that give them the right to discriminate on otherwise precluded grounds?

It is obvious that complete freedom of religion is impossible. It seems unlikely that many would agree to the importation of the Hindu caste system into this country, for example, nor the sort of physical punishments dispensed as criminal penalties in various theocracies around the world, of which "Dishonour killing" is one of the most appalling examples.

We therefore have no choice other than to pick and choose which religious traditions to allow. Or, to put it another way, the question is how, and to what extent, to tolerate intolerance. The articles within this part provide a few examples of that sort of picking and choosing in practice, and the final one sets out my general approach in opposition to that advanced by a well-known QC.

For most of the essays here I have deviated slightly from the path of the book to this point, in that there are fewer salacious personal details about the litigants. But I think the intellectual puzzles involved are interesting enough in themselves.

23. Disregarding the faith

Without question, religion and the law constitutes one of the most contentious issues in public debate in the present day. Criminal law is no exception, as illustrated by two high-profile cases from 2010.

The first was that of Shamso Miah, who punched a member of the public over an argument as to their respective places in a bank queue. The victim suffered a fractured jaw, and Miah subsequently pleaded guilty to assault occasioning actual bodily harm. Miss Cherie Booth QC, sitting as a part-time judge, imposed a sentence of two years' imprisonment, but proceeded to suspend the sentence on the basis that "[y]ou are a religious man and you know this is not acceptable behaviour."

Miss Booth's remarks were widely criticised at the time, and rightly so. They are illogical for a start: the fact that Miah knew his behaviour was wrong evidently did not stop him doing it. If anything, it should have been an aggravating factor, since it demonstrates he was able to assume full responsibility for his actions.

Moreover, belief in the concept of right and wrong is not the preserve of the religious. While the subject does not lend itself to brief summary, it can be observed that many great wrongs have been, and continue to be, committed in the name of religion. It is also true that many have been committed in the name of secular ideologies. The point is that making judgements about the relative merits of secular versus religious ideology or ethics is a philosophical minefield. It is no business of the courts, certainly not in straightforward criminal cases.

In any event, trying to adopt a religious exemption or mitigation for criminal conduct would be unworkable in a multi-faith (and perhaps predominantly secular) society such as the United Kingdom. There are too many

Published in *Criminal Law & Justice Weekly*, vol 175, 26 February 2011, p 124.

differing standards amongst too many faiths, never mind trying to define the concept of a religion to begin with.

It is true as a matter of historical observation that the common law and its values have a shared history with Christian ethics, and that the United Kingdom retains an established church. But the days of the common law being actively developed by religion have long passed, and the courts regularly reiterate (correctly) that they are a secular institution.

Judges should not, therefore, make any assumption about the character of defendants based upon their apparent religious beliefs, and in the particular case Miah's should have been of no mitigation or aggravation. The relevant factors were the same as any other defendant: prior convictions or absence thereof, and positive evidence of good or bad conduct.

Of course, good conduct may be motivated by religious belief, but that is neither here nor there. It is the conduct itself, not the informing belief, which constitutes the mitigating factor.

By the same reasoning, the religious beliefs of the victim are equally irrelevant, as should have been recognised in another highly publicised case, namely the attempted murder by Roshanara Choudhry of Stephen Timms MP.

According to the sentencing remarks, Choudhry had been indoctrinated into Islamic extremism, and stabbed Timms out of "revenge" for his having supported the Iraq War. The judge went on to contrast Choudhry's values unfavourably with Timms' strong Christian values, and when describing the latter lauded the historical relationship between Christianity and the common law.

It was right to observe that Timms was an innocent victim and that Choudhry was acting out of wholly inexcusable motives. Yet the purpose of the sentencing exercise was only to ascertain two things: first, whether the victim contributed towards the offence, and secondly, what other aggravating or mitigating factors applied to the defendant. Having established that Timms did nothing to provoke the attack, his other characteristics should have fallen away. The law does not evaluate the worthiness of criminal victims: an attempted murder is just as objectionable whether the victim is a selfish non-contributor to society or a genial philanthropist.

As to Choudhry, her beliefs were correctly judged to have been of no exculpatory or mitigating value whatsoever. They were, however, a factor in determining future risk – if she had carried out the attack in pursuance of her ideology and had no remorse or regret, then she was presumably likely to do it again.

Occasionally it is suggested that the presence of many faiths in the United Kingdom should be reflected in public institutions and processes. On the contrary, a separation of church and state is the only way that all beliefs (including non-beliefs) can be treated the same. This poses no threat to the survival of religion – quite the opposite. It ensures that no particular faith gains the favour of the state. And in the context of the criminal law it ensures that everyone is protected – and prosecuted – equally.

24. God behind bars

The relationship between religion and the law seems now to be a permanent feature of public life in the United Kingdom, to the point where it reminds one of the children's story about the magic pudding which, no matter how often it is eaten, always reforms in order to be eaten again.

One recent serving of the pudding concerns the right to practise religion in prison, which was the subject of *R (Bashir) v Independent Adjudicator* [2011] EWHC 1108 (Admin).

The claimant was required to provide a urine sample for testing for the use of controlled drugs in accordance with the policy in relation to mandatory drug testing contained in Prison Service Order 3601. The basis for the test was a suspicion that he had taken controlled substances. He was offered water before providing the sample, but refused on the ground that he was a devout Muslim who was fasting prior to a court hearing, as part of his religious preparation for the event. As a result of refusing water he was unable to provide a sufficient sample. He was charged with failing to obey a lawful rule contrary to r 51(22) of the Prison Rules 1999. He was convicted by a prison adjudicator and a penalty of 14 days' additional detention was imposed. The adjudicator held that the claimant was not fasting as part of either Ramadan or any other religious festival, and therefore requiring him to provide a sample had been "appropriate". The claimant applied by way of judicial review to quash the adjudicator's decision, contending that it had breached his right to practise his religion under Art 9 of the European Convention on Human Rights.

Judge Pelling found that the adjudicator's approach to Art 9 had been wrong; the correct approach required three questions: (i) whether the claimant's rights under

Co-written with Anne-Marie Forker, and published in *Criminal Law & Justice Weekly*, vol 175, 18 June 2011, p 373.

Art 9 were engaged; (ii) if so, whether there had been an interference with those rights; and (iii) if so, whether the interference was one that was both prescribed by law or necessary in the interests of public order, health or morals, and proportionate to the end pursued.

There was no real dispute both that Art 9 was engaged and that there had been an interference with those rights. Accordingly question (iii) formed the nub of the substantive challenge. Moreover, since the drug testing was prescribed by law and at least one of the other aspects of Art 9, the only aspect of (iii) that was in issue was whether it was proportionate to the end pursued.

Judge Pelling concluded that there had been no evidence before the adjudicator to suggest that it was proportionate to require all Muslim prisoners engaged in personal fasting to break that fast as and when required for the purposes of providing a sample regardless of the circumstances. The decision therefore had to be quashed.

We have no dispute with the judge's approach to Art 9. Rather, our difference is with the conclusion that the drug policy could potentially be a disproportionate interference with the claimant's rights. While the state is obliged to allow religious beliefs and practices, it is not obliged to make exceptions to the general law based on someone's religious beliefs – provided that the general law is not aimed at discriminating against or suppressing particular religions.

If it could have made no difference either to the state or to any private individual (including other prisoners), then we would have no objection to the state accommodating religious practices for prisoners. But making exceptions to the disciplinary regime – of which drug testing is at the core – is as unworkable as it is unfair. If one has an exception due to a fast, then why not some other activity? And, to ensure non-discrimination, non-religious beliefs of any particular prisoner would also have to be accommodated.

Religious exemptions are found elsewhere in the criminal law, such as s 139 of the Criminal Justice Act 1988 and ss 3 and 4 of the Offensive Weapons Act 1996, which allow Sikhs to carry the Kirpan on religious grounds. Is permitting this not increasing the likelihood of harm to others, something the criminal law aims to reduce? We are not suggesting that Sikhs are more likely than other groups to use knives in a criminal fashion, but rather that increasing the quantity of knives being carried by any section of society in the general public increases the risk of harm to others. Practising religion should be subject to the same standards as non-religious activities.

Contrary to the tabloid view that equality is somehow harmful to religion, we believe that excluding religion from public life is actually the best protection for religion, because it ensures all religions are treated equally.

25. No freedom of speech

When discussing religion and the law to this point, I have consistently argued for free speech and for a complete separation of church and state. The counterpoint that others have expressed is that religion has been subordinated to other rights such as gender and sexual orientation.

I would maintain that the approach I have advocated is equally applicable to defending religion. I have been asked for some examples. One obvious one concerns the sad tale of Harry Hammond's street protest in Bournemouth in October 2001 and his subsequent conviction for a public order offence. It also provides a classic freedom of speech case.

Hammond was born in 1932. The facts as found by the justices at his trial were as follows:

> "(a) [Mr Hammond] is an Evangelical Christian who has been a preacher for 20 years; he is a sincere man with deeply held religious beliefs and a desire to convert others to his way of thinking.
>
> (b) During the summer of 2001, [Mr Hammond] had a large double sided sign made bearing the words: 'Stop Immorality', 'Stop Homosexuality' and 'Stop Lesbianism' on each side and attached to a pole.
>
> (c) Prior to 13th October 2001, [Mr Hammond] had on at least one previous occasion preached whilst displaying the sign and had received a hostile reaction from members of the public, some of whom attempted to deface the sign and leading to one person trying to set it on fire.
>
> (d) During the afternoon of Saturday 13th October 2001, [Mr Hammond] travelled by bus to The Square, Bournemouth to preach with the sign; during the bus journey [Mr Hammond] covered the sign with a black plastic bin liner as he believed the sign might cause a

Published in *Criminal Law & Justice Weekly*, vol 175, 10 September 2011, p 527.

fracas if displayed inside the bus, because of the reaction he had previously received.

(e) On arriving at The Square, Bournemouth [Mr Hammond] positioned himself by a floral display near the Obscura cafe in the pedestrianised area of the town centre and began preaching holding the sign upright so that it was clearly visible to passers-by.

(f) A group of 30 to 40 people gathered around [Mr Hammond], arguing and shouting; some people in the crowd were angry, others were aggressive or distressed; some threw soil at the appellant; one person was hit over the head with the placard.

(g) Members of the public in the area at the time included: Miss Laura Backley, who was disgusted by the sign and found it annoying and, although not personally insulted, felt it was insulting to homosexuals and lesbians; Ms Michelle Watling who was upset, shocked and insulted by the sign; Miss Kerry Warden who found the sign insulting; Mr Sean Tapper, a homosexual, who lived in the street where the incident occurred and was personally insulted by the sign, upset and angry; and Mr Christopher Roger Mooney, Sean Tapper's partner, who found the sign insulting and distressing.

(h) At one point someone tried to pull the placard away from [Mr Hammond] during which [Mr Hammond] fell backwards to the ground; [Mr Hammond] got up again and continued with his preaching displaying the sign; at this point a member of the public poured water over [Mr Hammond's] head.

(i) Police Constables Gandy and Elliot attended the scene; Police Constable Gandy found the crowd to be agitated, angry and insulted.

(j) Police Constable Gandy spoke to [Mr Hammond] for several minutes and asked him to take the sign down and leave the area; [he] refused saying he was aware that his sign was insulting because he had had a similar reaction previously but that he intended to return the following Saturday to preach with the sign again.

(k) Police Constables Gandy and Elliott discussed the situation for several minutes, during which time they were approached by members of the public who were outraged that [Mr Hammond] had not been arrested.

(l) Police Constable Elliott was of the opinion that it was not necessary for the police to become involved in the incident or to take any action.

(m) Police Constable Gandy was of the view that the appellant was provoking violence and that it was not safe for her to leave the scene without intervening, and she therefore arrested [Mr Hammond] for breach of the peace."

Despite the fact that he seems to have been more on the receiving end of the violence, Hammond was arrested and charged with an offence under s 5 of the Public Order Act 1986. He was convicted, and then appealed by way of case stated to the Divisional Court. Sadly he died before the appeal could be heard, but the court went ahead in any event.

The court ruled that it was necessary for the prosecution to prove that the sign which Hammond was displaying was threatening, abusive or insulting and that it was within the hearing or sight of a person likely to be caused harassment, alarm or distress thereby. It was a defence for Hammond to prove that, nevertheless, his conduct was reasonable.

The court concluded, not without hesitation, that the conviction should stand. It held that (i) the words on the sign were capable of being held to be insulting, not least because they appeared to relate homosexuality and lesbianism to immorality; and (ii) notwithstanding familiar free speech arguments advanced on Hammond's behalf, it had been open to the justices to find his conduct unreasonable (see [2004] All ER (D) 50 (Jan)).

Harry Hammond's life and death therefore stand as part of the matrix of religion and the law, and freedom of expression generally.

Two things have been common to many cases in that matrix, including Hammond's. First, they concern people expressing genuine and deeply held beliefs that until very recently represented mainstream opinion in this country.

Secondly, for those involving homosexuality at least, they involve the expression or manifestation of opinions that would never be tolerated if they concerned other minority traits such as race.

Thus arises the key question at the heart of liberal philosophy: how to tolerate intolerance. In the context of free speech I have long endorsed the analogy advanced by Judge Richard Posner with America's cold war strategy. America's front line against the USSR, he observed, was not the Potomac but the Elbe. It was hoped that any conflict would be safely away from American soil, meaning ground could be ceded here and there without threatening their core interests.

Similarly, advocates of free speech argue for a wider protection than that strictly necessary to preserve values such as open and free political discussion, artistic freedom and personal fulfilment. They spend their time defending often offensive, sadistic, sordid or nonsensical manifestations of speech. By doing so they calculate that speech that is merely offensive, or indeed simply not finding favour with the political agenda of the government of the day, is never threatened.

Peter Tatchell, the inveterate homosexual rights campaigner, advanced a similar view when commenting on Hammond's case at the time of the original conviction:

> "Criminalising prejudiced opinions is a step too far. Where do you draw the line between legitimate robust criticism and illegitimate rank prejudice? The only circumstance where there is a clearly valid case for limiting freedom of speech is when it involves inciting violence."

No-one would have known better than Mr Tatchell that only a few years before it would have been gay rights campaigners like himself who were getting assaulted in town squares by angry crowds.

He would also have known that it was hardly likely, to put it mildly, that any passer-by would suddenly undergo a radical and irreversible change in their beliefs simply after seeing and hearing the sermons of Mr Hammond. I have seen many a street preacher but never an audience for one.

As much as I deplore homophobia, I remain uneasy with Harry Hammond being made a criminal. He simply outlived the mores of his time. I doubt all of us will be wholly immune from the same fate.

Afterword

I have since used the Hammond case in giving presentations on law and the legal system, as a good example of a classic free speech question. Each time I have been hardened in my opinion that he was wrongly convicted. The reason is simple. No-one would think that if he had been protesting in favour of gay rights or racial equality decades before that he should have been guilty if the same public fracas had ensued (which it probably would have done). The only distinction between such hypothetical examples and the actual Hammond case is the message he sought to make – his was against modern conceptions of human rights, not for. In other words, the only distinction was his opinion, not his actions, and a free society does not criminalise opinions.

26. France's burqa ban: the legal implications

On 11 April a new law took effect in France, banning the wearing of the burqa in public. Though there are no plans for any equivalent law in Britain, it would be idle to pretend the controversy has no relevance here.

At first sight it seems absurd that the state should regulate what clothing people choose to wear. Freedom of expression and freedom of religion require – as a strong starting point at least – the ability to display religious symbols and comply with religious tenets as to dress in public.

As ever, things are not that simple. The British state already regulates what people wear in public, for example by precluding indecent exposure. The limits of that regulation are always disputed but there is no argument for it to be repealed in toto. Further, wearing clothes with racist or otherwise offensive slogans might attract a public order prosecution. Accordingly, banning the burqa in public would not be a wholly unprecedented measure.

Whilst many might wear the burqa voluntarily, both by way of adherence to their religion and perhaps also a rejection of the oversexualisation of women in Western society, others may be forced to wear it. The new French law acknowledges the difference between the two situations: the wearer will face a fine of €450 and/or a course in "citizenship", but a man who forces a woman to become a wearer will incur a fine of €30,000 and imprisonment. One would presume in the latter situation that there would be no prosecution of the woman.

It is not relevant that very few women (under 2,000 according to one report) actually wear the burqa in France

Published on *Halsbury's Law Exchange* on 13 April 2011. This post received more hits than any other I wrote for the site.

(though if anything that is a reason in favour of the ban). Nor is the French government's actual motivation for the ban (the subject of some speculation) relevant to whether it is morally justifiable or not.

All that said, I see no case at present for a ban in the UK. The main problem is that there are no cogent statistics showing how many women wear the item voluntarily as opposed to under duress. Given the inherent difficulties in compiling any such statistics (someone in an abusive relationship will probably not feel able to answer freely, even in an anonymous survey), it would seem unlikely there ever will be – though if anything that lends support to a ban. More importantly, however, anyone in an oppressive relationship will not be saved from abuse simply by the law preventing her from wearing a burqa in public – indeed, it risks making her a criminal as well as a victim. There is certainly a justification for the state acting against an oppressive husband who forces his wife to wear the burqa, but a burqa ban will not of itself release anyone from oppression and in any event there are already laws against domestic abuse, as well as private and public forms of assistance for its victims.

Arguments about whether the Koran really does mandate the wearing of the burqa or whether the item is simply a manifestation of extremism or a non-religious cultural practice do not settle the issue. The state is not in a position to adjudicate theological disputes, and freedom of religion precludes it from doing so in any event.

In essence, if a woman has been forced to wear the burqa by an oppressive husband she should have the right and the means (provided by the state) to leave that relationship if she wishes. If she has chosen to wear it voluntarily, her motivation – religious, cultural, fashion or other – is no-one else's business. The resources of the state should be directed at identifying and addressing domestic abuse, not arresting people on a speculative basis because of their clothing.

Notwithstanding the above conclusion, there are particular circumstances in which both the state and private entities can and should ban the burqa (and various other items of clothing, both religious and non-religious). First, state schools should be permitted to ban religious clothing as part of the separation of church and state.

Secondly, banks, airports and other places with serious security concerns should be entitled to require burqas to be removed on their premises, as they do for anything else covering the face such as motorcycle helmets.

Thirdly, the rule of open justice – a cornerstone of the common law – should trump the right to wear a burqa. Accordingly, a witness may not insist on wearing the burqa whilst giving evidence, nor should the court be cleared whilst she is doing so. The present guidance to the contrary is, I suggest, unlawful.

Finally, I would hesitate before condemning the French, despite disagreeing with the ban. There is much to be admired in the French concept of *laïcité*, as foreshadowed by what I have written in earlier articles about law and religion. As a manifestation of that concept a ban may well be more justifiable.

Afterword

The burqa ban was later cited in a letter to the *Times* as an example of France's failed policy of integration of immigrants. This seemed to me to miss the point slightly, so I wrote the following response, which was published on the letters page on 9 January 2012:

> "Mr Edward Carey (letter, 6 January) criticises France's integration policy, and offers the burqa ban as example of its flaws. It might be said that the problem in France is not the policy as such, but the failure to implement it. A glance at the ethnic ghettos in France and lack of minority representation amongst the French great and the good suggests that France might demand that immigrants become French but too often declines to treat them as such.
>
> The burqa ban was implemented not simply as part of a policy towards the immigrant community but rather the French concept of laïcité, or separation of church and state. I do not think the ban was a necessary consequence

> of laïcité, but nonetheless that concept if implemented consistently would apply equally to immigrants and indigenous alike, and would have avoided many of the disputes in Britain of the past few years about religious exemptions for minorities."

Not all have the same view either of integration of immigrants or the separation of church and state, as we will now see.

27. Aiden O'Neill QC on religion and the law

Mr Aiden O'Neill QC has written an interesting counterpoint to recent developments in law and religion (http://ukhumanrightsblog.com/2011/03/29/squaring-equality-with-religion).

His view deserves a response.

Mr O'Neill summarises the present state of the law as follows:

> "The courts analyse such cases from a discrimination law perspective by asking whether a person without religiously based views would have been permitted to act in any of these ways. If both a religious and a non-religious person would not have been permitted to do these things, then there is no discrimination on grounds of religion or belief."

He criticises this approach on the basis that there is a distinction between informed religious beliefs and secular beliefs; the former, he argues, are:

> "intimately tied into the moral values to which [the religious] would adhere, by word and deed. Failing to act on those beliefs is not an option for the religious, because a failure so to act expresses for them a denial of their beliefs."

There are several responses. First, it would be of small consolation to someone on the receiving end of what would otherwise be unlawful discrimination to be told that the discriminator was sincerely following a prescribed moral code. I doubt, for example, whether someone deemed untouchable by hardline adherents of the Hindu caste system, or excluded by followers of the former Dutch Reformed Church, would have any sympathy for Mr O'Neill QC's views. That those are

Published on *Halsbury's Law Exchange* on 5 April 2011.

extreme examples does not change the fundamental principle of non-discrimination.

Secondly, while it is true that some religious people who have been in the courts recently may have been genuine adherents of a mainstream religion who were acting according to deeply held beliefs, others seeking a religious-based exemption from anti-discrimination laws might simply be religious adherents of convenience, who offer a religious belief as a straw defence to justify bigotry held on other grounds. The courts are ill-equipped to judge anyone's piety.

Thirdly, one would also have to define a religion, another exercise courts are not well placed to undertake.

Fourthly, there would have to be a list of acceptable or unacceptable religious beliefs for the purposes of legal exemption. No-one would support on religious grounds stoning someone to death for adultery, or withdrawing a female child from education, or forced marriages, or female genital mutilation. But compiling such a list would be an invidious task and bound to be over-or under-inclusive. Alternatively, some principles would have to be formulated for the courts to implement on a case-by-case basis, which would likely lead to unacceptable uncertainty.

Mr O'Neill argues that, on his analysis, being religious is akin to having a disability: the law requires that account be taken of disability and appropriate measures taken to place the disabled on an equal footing with those without that disability. He says the same should occur for religions. The analogy is false. For a start, there is no choice about having a disability, whereas people often abandon or otherwise modify their religious beliefs.

Mr O'Neill would doubtless respond that for many it is not at all possible to change their beliefs, still less is it reasonable for the law to require them to do so. Yet the analogy still does not hold up: there is nothing about having a disability which affects anyone else's rights, still less anyone else's right not to be discriminated against. One person having a disability is irrelevant to anyone else's right not to be discriminated against on the ground of race, gender, age or sexual orientation, for example – no reasonable adjustment would have anything to do with those grounds.

Underlying Mr O'Neill's thesis is the assumption that religious beliefs are of a different nature to secular beliefs of any form and, he inevitably has to argue, somehow more deserving of the law's protection. He contends that

> "there can be no proper comparison between those who would discriminate on grounds of a religiously informed conscience, and those who so act simply from unthinking incoherent prejudice or bigotry."

With respect, that argument is not sustainable. Some religions might constitute deeply held belief systems with centuries of provenance. Others might be bizarre and extremist offshoots. Recent cases have shown the difficulties inherent in distinguishing one from the other. Moreover, someone might write a scholarly thesis on the dangers of religion and seek to exclude religious people from their public establishment accordingly – not all who discriminate on secular grounds are unthinking bigots.

The overarching principle regarding religion and the law is that one is entitled to respect for the right to hold beliefs, but not those beliefs themselves. Just because a person is entitled to hold a belief does not mean that another person has to pay for it, or suffer unlawful discrimination because of it.

Part VI: Public Law – The State in a State

Public law concerns the business of government and its relationship with its citizens. Three rather different issues arise in the three cases considered in this part.

The first is the latest attempt (of many attempts) by the government to simplify the tax laws. It is a relief that the recently established Office of Tax Simplification is composed of eminent tax lawyers giving their time for free. But it will not stop the uneasy sense that it is not in the interest of tax lawyers drafting legislation to make tax understandable for anyone else (even other tax lawyers) because they make a living selling advice on it.

Even if tax draftsmen are in fact happy to do so, the real problem lies with the desire of the government to buy votes and otherwise manipulate behaviour by providing tax exemptions left, right and centre for those with whom it is trying to curry favour.

The second and third articles have had so much media coverage an introduction is not particularly needed. The first concerns an MP's prosecution for expenses, and the second the right of prisoners to vote. I have gone with the view of the majority of the public in both cases – against the MPs and against the prisoners. Seemingly the majority of human rights lawyers are not with me on the second, though most are on the first. Readers can make up their own mind ...

28. A simple title, an impossible task

Today (20 July 2010) the Chancellor George Osborne has announced that he is setting up an "Office for Tax Simplification" (OTS).

One has some sympathy for the members of this new office, whom so far include amongst their number former Conservative MP and Treasury minister Michael Jack, as Chairman, and John Whiting, formerly of PricewaterhouseCoopers, who is tax director at the Chartered Institute of Taxation, as Director. Each has just been despatched to legislative drafting's equivalent of the Eastern front but, honourably, neither will be paid.

We have been here before, of course. The Finance Bill of 1986 prompted much grumbling from solicitors and accountants due to its complexity. A decade later, with characteristically bland understatement, the Inland Revenue reported that the language of the existing law "could be simplified". The then-Chancellor, Ken Clarke MP, had a go at this with a rewriting project. It began unpromisingly with Mr Clarke offering that the project was as ambitious as "translating *War and Peace* into lucid Swahili". He then admitted that that, too, was an understatement, since *War and Peace* was a quarter the length of the tax law as it then stood (1,500 pages for the Russian novel versus 6,000 pages for UK tax lawyers) and "hadn't been written by a Tolstoy". Former finance draftsman Francis Bennion later observed in an article in the *New Law Journal* (vol 151, 26 January 2001, p 104): "He might have added that neither is *War and Peace* a palimpsest of a thousand disconnected fragments from different years ..."

By 2001, following a change of government, the project had managed to come up with the Capital Allowances Bill,

Originally written as an internal LNUK blog.

which weighed in at a mere 903 pages for just one area of tax law. Mr Jack was still an MP at the time and told the House he was pleased with the effort, though Mr John Redwood MP couldn't resist asking whether he thought Ken Clarke would have been happy with the outcome in the light of his introductory remarks in 1996.

On the reformers pressed and, among various other efforts, six years later we had the Income Tax Act 2007. One objective of this was to consolidate existing legislation and hence make it easier to find, though it was also hoped that it would be "easier to understand" – which is not the same thing. The Act amounted to almost 1,000 sections and, in a depressing act of symmetry, in the subsequent three years almost 1,000 amendments have been passed, leaving little of the original wording intact. I wonder if anyone's found anything easier as a result.

Ken Clarke, long thought politically extinct, is now back with us as Justice Minister, and so it would be a useful time to ask him Mr Redwood's question again.* Given that we have gone from 6,000 pages in 1996 to 11,000 in 2010 we can probably assume he wouldn't have been happy in 1996 and isn't happy now. He along with the rest of us will be wishing Mr Osborne's simplifying office all the best in their endeavours, but unless the fundamental reason behind tax complexity is addressed their task is impossible, and will have the same outcome as all the other reforming efforts already mentioned.

That fundamental reason was expressed in one sentence by Mr Bennion in the article quoted above: "It is policy that produces complexity". The UK government has always used the tax system, and always will, not simply as a means to raise revenue but to try and engineer what it considers socially desirable outcomes. Hence in capital allowances it is forever trying to discriminate between different classes of assets. VAT law, too, is absolutely riddled with exemptions dating back to its introduction. All one can say is that they started as they meant to go on. A former Parliamentary Draftsman once

* Ken Clarke since the time of writing has been replaced as Justice Minister

told (*Times Letters*, 13 June 2006) of how the government of the day presented his office with an absurd task by wanting an exemption for VAT for "the working man's fish and chips". The results of the effort to provide for such an exemption in a legally satisfying form are still with us today.

Much later a similarly absurd complication was unleashed by Parliament when it decided that the other form of chip, that formerly known as crisps, were a bad thing, and therefore had to be exempted from a general exemption. This led to litigation over whether or not the well known Pringles product were actually potato crisps, and accordingly exempted, which in turn depended on whether Pringles were similar to potato crisps and made from the potato (for the record they were, despite having less actual potato content than other crisps: see *Procter & Gamble UK v Revenue and Customs Commrs* [2009] EWCA Civ 407, [2009] All ER (D) 177 (May)). One might also mention the dispute over whether Jaffa cakes were biscuits or cakes, or the classification of Marks and Spencer teacakes ...

When, therefore, not if, the OTS fails in its task, is it too much to hope that anyone will take heed of the fundamental problem?

Afterword

The Times letter referred to above was in response to a shibboleth offered by the-then Constitutional Affairs Minister Harriet Harman. Ms Harman said that a new bill was "for the first time" being offered in "plain English" as well as the normal legalese. She led the public to believe that the two versions would appear side by side and at long last the public could actually grasp what an Act of Parliament meant without any professional advice.

In fact no such "plain English" version existed. All that happened was that the usual explanatory notes were more extensive than normal. This was no great surprise – imagine the potential for confusion and argument if there were to be two versions of the same Act. (Or ask any

New Zealand lawyer what complications followed two versions – one in English and the other in Maori – of the country's most important constitutional document, the Treaty of Waitangi ...)

Ms Harman, a solicitor by trade, should have grasped the point. One is entitled to draw adverse conclusions from the fact that she did not.

There is a second point too, namely whether it is really possible to draft legal documents including statutes in "plain English". Of course there is always room for improvement in drafting and anyone could come up with historic examples of hopelessly badly drafted sections, or even whole acts. Lord Justice Rose once had this to say about a particularly egregious example:

> "So, yet again, the courts are faced with a sample of the deeply confusing provisions of the Criminal Justice Act 2003, and the satellite statutory instruments to which it is giving stuttering birth. The most inviting course for this court to follow, would be for its members, having shaken their heads in despair to hold up their hands and say: 'the Holy Grail of rational interpretation is impossible to find.' But it is not for us to desert our judicial duty, however lamentably others have legislated. But, we find little comfort or assistance in the historic canons of construction for determining the will of Parliament which were fashioned in a more leisurely age and at a time when elegance and clarity of thought and language were to be found in legislation as a matter of course rather than exception."

But there are also limits. Shortly after Ms Harman's announcement I also had a letter published in the Times (June 17, 2006):

> "Sir, The Constitutional Affairs Minister Harriet Harman seems to have forgotten that legislation is complex because human activity, which it seeks to regulate, is also complex, and as a result law is a specialist subject, just as with architecture or medicine. The only way that a paper on new heart transplant techniques could be rendered intelligible would be if the reader had studied the subject

> — and was hence no longer a member of 'the public' — or if the paper were simplified to the point where it was more or less completely unhelpful to a surgeon.
>
> The example you give of an apparently plain English provision bears this out. You report that the Offences Against the Persons Act 1861 states: 'It is an offence to cause a riot.'
>
> Perfectly plain, until someone is charged under the section and it has to be determined what 'caused' and 'riot' mean in context."

I always liked the definition in s 13(1) of the Finance Act 1940 of a short lease:

> "'short lease' means a lease which is not a long lease."

I cannot resist adding the Statutory Instrument nominated by Lord Justice Sedley as the most baffling of all, the Nuts (Unground) (Other than Groundnuts) (Amendment) Order:

> "In the Nuts (Unground) (Other than Groundnuts) Order, the expression 'nuts' shall have reference to such nuts, other than groundnuts, as would but for this amending Order not qualify as nuts (unground) (other than groundnuts) by reason of their being nuts (unground)."
>
> ("This beats me", 35 *London Review of Books* 7 (2 April 1998))

I would finally observe that despite all of the above there is one thing Ms Harman and her colleagues could do to make legislation much more comprehensible to all concerned – pass less of it.

29. A modern scandal

On 7 January, Mr David Chaytor became the first MP to be sentenced in relation to an offence committed in respect of parliamentary expenses. His guilty plea followed a preliminary ruling by the Supreme Court that the system of expenses did not attract parliamentary privilege (as established by Art 9 of the Bill of Rights 1689), nor did Parliament itself have exclusive jurisdiction over the issue. The case is noteworthy, if primarily because of the high degree of public interest rather than any new legal principle.

Of the courts involved, it was the Court of Appeal who most invoked the spirit of Denning at the constitutional pulpit. It stated that parliamentary privilege was the "bedrock of our democracy", and that the finest example of the principle in action was Leo Amery's speech in the Commons in 1940. Following the severe military reverses of that year, Amery launched a direct attack on the incumbent Prime Minister, Neville Chamberlain, concluding with Cromwell's famous exhortation "in the name of God, go".

I would certainly agree with the Court of Appeal about the significance of Amery's speech. Had he made the same speech in most other countries, not to say Hitler's Reichstag, they would have been about the last words he ever spoke.

There was, incidentally, a tragic irony from Amery's personal point of view, as his elder son Jack went on to make pro-German broadcasts from Berlin on a similar line to those of William Joyce, whom I wrote about in chapter 11. As with Joyce, Jack Amery was executed for treason after the war. He also recommended PG Wodehouse to the Abwehr, which has led to some casting much harsher aspersions upon Wodehouse than I did earlier in the book.

Published in *Criminal Law & Justice Weekly*, vol 175, 5 February 2011, p 73.

Back to the *Chaytor* case. On appeal the Supreme Court reiterated the importance of Art 9, perhaps with fewer rhetorical flourishes but with no lesser emphasis.

There is accordingly no doubting the importance of Parliament being a forum where everything is up for the most robust debate, even if outside the House it might carry legal consequences in libel or worse. To the extent that MPs might abuse that privilege, it is a matter for the House itself to control—usually in the form of the Speaker—with no recourse to the courts.

Moreover, parliamentary business extends beyond simply what is said in either House, and other activities may therefore attract the privilege defence. As Lord Phillips stated, the test is whether impugned actions fall within "parliamentary proceedings" because of their connection to the Houses and their committees, which in turn concerns the nature of that connection and any impact of a prosecution on the essential business of Parliament.

He went on to hold that expense claims failed that test and therefore did not attract privilege.

The second limb of the defence was based on the slightly archaic sounding "exclusive cognisance" of Parliament; in other words, whether Parliament alone had jurisdiction to deal with its own affairs.

As with Art 9, the boundaries of the defence are imprecise, but Lord Phillips was clear that "the mere fact that a crime has been committed within these precincts [of Parliament] is no bar to the jurisdiction of the criminal courts", and that Parliament itself had never challenged that proposition. Further, although a prosecution would ordinarily require the co-operation of Parliament, that was not essential.

Accordingly, the trial of Chaytor and the other defendants was allowed to continue. Of course that was the only acceptable result. Either the MPs took more than they were entitled to or they did not. It was crucial for that question to be decided in the ordinary courts, with the same rights and same procedures to which anyone else would be entitled. Nothing less would suffice for justice to be seen to be done, and for public confidence in the institution of Parliament to be restored. As Denning himself once put it (quoting Thomas Fuller):

> "Be you never so high, the law is above you" (*Gouriet v Union of Postal Workers* [1977] 1 All ER 696 at 718).

That said, any wider constitutional significance of the case can be downplayed. Contrary to some published opinion, it says nothing about the relationship of the Supreme Court and Parliament. The Appellate Committee of the House of Lords would certainly have reached the same conclusion (as had the lower courts already), and moreover the actual trials will not take place in the Supreme Court itself but rather the Crown Court.

One final point. The last word on the affair will not be the preserve of the criminal courts, but rather the court of public opinion. MPs and everyone else involved in the system would do well to act accordingly.

Afterword

Chaytor and his co-defendants were duly tried, as were a number of others, and several ended up with terms of imprisonment. I have to say though that the whole affair appears just as squalid in hindsight as it did at the time. Four aspects grated on me. First, the MPs all defended themselves on the basis that they did not "break any rules". Leaving aside any appeal to morality or a sense of public service, it is far from clear that rules were not broken. The House of Commons' "Green Book", which governed claims at the material time, set out a number of detailed rules. It was these that the MPs claimed they had followed, and perhaps they were correct in most cases. However, the detailed rules were expressly stated to be subject to a set of overriding principles. These included:

- Claims should be above reproach.
- Claims must only be made for expenditure that it was necessary for an MP to incur to ensure that he or she could properly perform his or her parliamentary duties.

- MPs must ensure that claims do not give rise to, or give the appearance of giving rise to, an improper personal financial benefit to themselves or anyone else.
- MPs are committed to openness about what expenditure has been incurred and for what purposes.
- MPs should avoid purchases which could be seen as extravagant or luxurious.

Needless to say most of the claims which received press attention broke at least some of the above principles, and many broke them all. Certainly the fourth principle did for the argument that house renovations and the like were MPs' "private business".

The second nauseating aspect was that, for everyone else, any expenses that could not be shown to be absolutely necessary for business purposes would be considered as income by the Revenue, and taxed accordingly. Many MPs seemed unconcerned.

Thirdly, all the money spent on second homes so that MPs from outside London (or not very far outside, in some cases) could have access to Westminster could not be justified once the MPs in question lost their seat or retired. In each instance, therefore, the second home should then have been sold and the taxpayer repaid not only the amount spent but a proportionate share of the capital gain made on the house (or the taxpayer could take a share of the loss in a housing depression, if anyone remembers what those are).

Fourthly, despite the fact that the system was shown to be fundamentally flawed, both in theory and in execution, the best that anyone did about it was fiddle around and produce a revised version of exactly the same thing, showing a thoroughly depressing lack of imagination.

The fundamental flaw to which I referred was this: any system which operates by people making claims and then hoping to get them approved, but with no restriction on the amount that might be claimed or penalty for having a number of claims refused, gives every encouragement to people to keep on shoving in claim after claim for anything and everything. Any rational, profit-maximising individual would do nothing else.

There are many alternatives. For example, MPs could simply have a fixed sum added to their salaries, to be spent on support staff, travelling expenses or whatever, but no more. Then they would have every incentive to economise.

All the talk about second homes and travel expenses was predicated on the assumption that MPs actually needed to be in any particular physical place at any particular time. In the age of smartphones, videoconferencing and unlimited broadband access, however, that assumption is very hard to justify.

Alternatively, let us assume that it is for a variety of reasons desirable for MPs to be physically present in the Houses of Parliament. Let us also assume that it would be unfair for MPs outside the M25 to be saddled with the extra costs of travelling to and staying in London. Then, one could build a hall of residence for those MPs (with a grander name if one prefers). It could be a modern, furnished and serviced apartment block next to the Palace of Westminster. It would cost a tiny fraction of the amount spent on second homes, the security costs would be far lower as there would only be one building to protect, and MPs would have no more and no less than they needed.

No doubt MPs would feel demeaned. No doubt no-one else would care, but in any event I would observe that a number of large city law firms have dormitories on their premises, together with a few ancillary services such as a canteen and laundry service. These are provided for partners working overtime on large deals. If it is good enough for millionaire city lawyers, it should be good enough for MPs. If the apartment block was within walking distance from the Houses of Parliament (perhaps with an underground tunnel to reduce security costs and provide disabled access), it would slash travelling expenses as well.

But such a suggestion was hardly mentioned, and never in a serious vein. Such is the lack of lateral thinking (or perhaps it is the presence of self interest) amongst our political masters.

30. Prisoner voting and the power of Strasbourg

Frances Crook, the (superbly named) Director of the Howard League for Penal Reform, has argued passionately on prisoners' voting rights and the European Court of Human Rights (the ECtHR) (*Criminal Law & Justice Weekly*, vol 175, p 82). Both issues, still regularly appearing in headlines, deserve further comment.

Ms Crook describes the right to vote as "fundamental", without defining the term. Yet no-one suggests that children or the clinically insane should have the franchise. "Fundamental", therefore, cannot mean "universal".

The rationale for withholding the vote from children or the insane is that both lack the intellectual maturity to make any meaningful contribution to the democratic process. One could anticipate a chaotic result from the aggregate of their votes. Further, children acquire the vote when they become adults (as would the mentally ill if cured), so it is wrong to consider them excluded as a class.

What then of prisoners? Obviously, commission of a crime does not of itself rob one of the intellectual capacity to vote. Nor is disenfranchisement a necessary component of imprisonment. We have moved on since the days in which prison constituted "civic death". Moreover, allowing prisoners the vote would assist them in developing the notion of participating in society, a key step in rehabilitation.

As against that, prisoners already have the right to vote – before they choose to become criminals. They will regain the right once freed. To call them "vulnerable", as some have, sits uneasily with the fact that many are imprisoned to protect the public. Rehabilitation may be

Published in *Criminal Law & Justice Weekly*, vol 175, 9 April 2011, p 229.

the ideal outcome of prison, but there has to be some element of punishment as well.

The notion of the social contract entails accepting the protection and benefits conferred by the state, but in exchange for duties on the part of the citizen. Rights should not exist without responsibilities. Foremost among responsibilities is the criminal law. Having chosen to break that law, prisoners are on shaky grounds demanding the right to have a say in making it for everyone else.

Then there is the ECtHR's compromise in *Hirst v the United Kingdom (No 2)* [2005] ECHR 681, which precludes a blanket ban but not necessarily a more limited restriction (although the ECtHR has arguably gone further since). The main point, however, is that the issue of prisoners' voting is far from clear cut. That being so, we come to the second question, namely whether Parliament or the ECtHR should ultimately decide.

Ms Crook argues "the law is the law": Parliament agreed to the ECtHR's jurisdiction and is therefore stuck with it. To pick or choose which rulings to follow would clearly breach the rule of law.

With this I agree, but that is not to deny that there are serious questions about the ECtHR. Its appointments process has been criticised as too political, with some judges insufficiently experienced and some not even fluent in the relevant languages. It is also a triumph of tokenism over logic that small political enclaves have equal representation with the likes of Germany and Britain.

The ECtHR was established to be a check on national governments. But what if the ECtHR itself starts exceeding its authority, or regularly produces decisions of unacceptably poor quality? It may become so aggressively expansionist – or simply incompetent – that the UK has to leave if it is unable to persuade fellow members of the need for reform. There is already cause for concern given that the ECtHR's critics include someone of the reputation and standing of Lord Hoffmann. A "living instrument" the Convention might be, but it should not be a licence for the ECtHR to micromanage national legal systems.

Nevertheless, those are reasons for reform, not excuses to pick and choose which currently binding rulings to follow. The fact is that Britain has to accord the ECtHR's decisions the authority conferred by the appropriate constitutional documents which it has willingly signed, unless and until it unsigns them.

This involves some niceties regarding the doctrine of parliamentary supremacy. As with membership of the EU itself, the most satisfactory analysis would perhaps be to say that Parliament has, for the duration of Britain's membership, delegated sovereignty to the necessary extent, or accepted a restriction on its own powers – although it still retains the power to withdraw at any time and reassert its former constitutional position.

Currently the Supreme Court is trying to resist another of the ECtHR's decisions in the *Horncastle* case. It seems improbable that it will be in a better position to do so than Parliament, but it is another indication that the controversy over Britain's relationship with Strasbourg is set to increase.

As divisive as the issues are, one can be against enfranchising prisoners but in favour of complying with the law as it presently stands. Equally, one can be in favour of allowing prisoners to vote and of demanding reform of the ECtHR – indeed, logic suggests that the ECtHR's supporters should also be the strongest advocates for its reform.

Part VII: The Press and the Public

A free and open press is a fundamental part of a free and democratic society. At the same time, all of us have aspects of our lives we consider private, and would like the press to respect that and the law to enforce it. This part has a few observations on how the law has tried to balance those two competing considerations over the years.

The first article contains a few observations on the press and the courts generally, garnered from the years I have spent knocking around with the court system in one capacity or another. There are some lighter touches, but the underlying point – the value of the press in keeping judges and lawyers honest – is of the utmost seriousness.

The rest of this part of the book concerns cases which had to determine whether there should be an actionable right to privacy when the press goes too far. The first two cases, both from New Zealand, I picked out because I remembered from law school days the interesting dilemmas they posed. The unfortunate Mr Tucker's life literally depended upon him keeping his unsavoury past quiet, since he needed donations from the general public to pay for specialist medical treatment. In the second case, by contrast, the aggrieved Mr Bradley really ought to have developed a thicker skin before wasting court time complaining about his family grave appearing in a splatter horror film.

The next two cases are both from the United Kingdom. Naomi Campbell's case was perhaps the most important early decision in this area of the law. Given that she was up against a well-known tabloid newspaper edited at the time by one Piers Morgan, her chances of keeping much of her private life under wraps was, to say the least, up against it, but nevertheless she fought all the way to Europe to defend her right to privacy.

Then there is the case of Prince Charles and the disloyal subject who leaked extracts from his private diary to the press. I was not surprised at all about the outcome of the Prince's action for breach of confidence, but in view of the strong opposing opinion of Lord Pannick QC it is worth examining the case and its merits. I have then added an afterword with some speculation about how privacy law may develop – or rather, be forced to develop.

31. The shrinking of Fleet Street

The Fleet Street hack is a vocation steeped in tradition, which may properly be called noble despite its share of ignoble practitioners and conventions. For any number of years journalists have been filling press benches at the Royal Courts of Justice, column inches in the dailies and glasses in the pubs, as they chronicle the drama, misery and other facets of humanity that every piece of litigation evokes in one form or another.

Rumpole also called himself a hack, and famously enjoyed a glass of *Chateau Thames Embankment*. But even inveterate junior counsel who have spent a lifetime not earning silk or becoming head of chambers would be going some to match the scribes in the work/life imbalance. Belting out copy in time for an after work rendezvous at *El Vinos*, the *Seven Stars* or the *Knights' Templar* remains the stock in trade of any self-regarding hack. Bonus points are earned by doing it in reverse order. Oscar Wilde's quip that work is the curse of the drinking classes has rarely been so apposite.

It has long been thus, although in the old days there was more smoking, fewer women and no blackberries. Until recently the only information web on which the hacks were able to rely was not worldwide at all, but rather in an invisible set of strands crossing the aforementioned public houses. The scene was quite beautifully set by Griffith LJ in a passage which surprisingly dates from only 30 years ago despite being redolent with the sort of chauvinism that most probably associate with a much earlier era (*Gill and another v El Vino Co Ltd* [1983] QB 425, 431):

> "El Vino's is no ordinary wine bar, it has become a unique institution in Fleet Street. Every day it is thronged with journalists, solicitors, barristers exchanging the gossip of the day. No doubt it is the source of many false rumours which have dashed the hopes of many an aspirant to a

Published on *Lexisweb* in October 2010.

High Court appointment. Now if a man wishes to take a drink in El Vino's he can drink, if he wishes, by joining the throng which crowds round the bar and there he can join his friends and pick up, no doubt, many an interesting piece of gossip, particularly if he is a journalist. Or, if he wishes, he can go and sit down at one of the two tables that are on the right immediately behind the main door of the premises. Thirdly, if he wishes, he can pass through the partition and enter the little smoking room at the back, which is equipped with a number of tables and chairs. But there is no doubt that very many men choose to stand among the throng drinking at the bar.

But if a woman wishes to go to El Vino's, she is not allowed to join the throng before the bar. She must drink either at one of the two tables on the right of the entrance, or she must pass through the throng and drink in the smoking room at the back. There is no doubt whatever that she is refused facilities that are accorded to men, and the only question that remains is: is she being treated less favourably than men? I think that permits of only one answer: of course she is. She is not being allowed to drink where she may want to drink, namely standing up among the many people gathered in front of the bar. There are many reasons why she may want to do so. Her friends may be there. She may not want to break them up and force them to move to some other part of the premises where she is permitted to drink. Or she may wish, if she is a journalist, to join a group in the hope of picking up the gossip of the day. If male journalists are permitted to do it, why shouldn't she? If she is denied it she is being treated less favourably than her male colleagues.

For the reasons given by Eveleigh L.J., I think the judge in the county court was distracted by the authorities which were cited to him dealing with the meaning of 'detriment' in section 6 (2) (b). Furthermore, I cannot regard this as de minimis; women are denied a facility which may be of particular importance to a journalist."

Nowadays journalists are as mixed in terms of gender as any other profession, although I offer no comment on residual misogyny. The utility of *El Vinos* as a source of information has only been slightly displaced by the internet and it is not for luddite reasons that one suspects virtual drinking establishments or social networking sites will never supplant the real thing for the hacks.

All that said, it seems as though legal journalists of whatever variety are a fading breed, according to David Banks in an article in the *Guardian* (19 October 2010). Mr Banks argues that with fewer local courts to sustain local journalists and, more worryingly, the preference of modern editors for "churnalism" – by which I imagine Mr Banks is referring to the bland non-news produced by the many blood relatives of Private Eye's Phil Space – the days of reporters sitting patiently through the many boring days and boring cases to find the gems of public interest are fast diminishing.

There are a number of serious points here. One recalls Lord Hewart's famous dictum that:

> "it is not merely of some importance but is of fundamental importance that justice should not only be done, but should manifestly and undoubtedly be seen to be done".

That is the cornerstone of English justice. It is reflected in the rules regarding open courts, the few exceptions to which are always the subject of robust debate. It is the means by which judges – unelected law makers who wield great power – are kept in democratic check: indeed it has long been observed that judges are the only public servants who make (almost) every decision in public, and whose every decision is reviewable.

Yet only the tiniest proportion of the general public has the time and the inclination to sit in court observing cases. Almost all who do are only there because they have an interest in the outcome. The rest rely, naturally enough, on the media to inform them of what happens in the courts. It follows that the role of the journalist is one of the highest public importance. Fewer journalists means fewer reports which means a weakening of that vital role.

It is true that not all of what journalists publish about court proceedings concerns important legal developments; they of course want the drama, the gossip, the sleaze and any other aspect of human foibles. Reports of any "celebrity" are likely to concern their appearance and demeanour in the court rather than whether the law on privacy has been correctly applied. And indeed the local gazettes and newsletters, whose reporters might attend the local courts, or who buy copy from freelance hacks in the Royal Courts in London, are equally likely to be more concerned with the antecedent regional soap operas that gave rise to litigation in the first place, rather than any actual legal point.

Arguably none of this can be described as being of public interest, in the sense of something that truly affects the public rather than just what the public happens to be interested in. However true that might be, it cannot detract from the importance of legal journalists. Their mere presence ensures a watchdog for anything untoward that might happen in court. Judges who fall asleep, counsel who lose their temper, jurors who behave improperly will all quickly supplant the worthless gossip in the journalists' attention, and be brought to book in the court of public opinion accordingly. Nor is it necessarily a bad thing that anyone who attends court has to accept that they are going to be the object of public scrutiny.

Other countries tightly control the press when it comes to court procedures, others may not have any legal impediments but, due to lack of resources and the same sort of press tradition, have proportionately fewer journalists. None may be admired in that respect.

One final point. The role of reporting law is not that of those variously described as journalists, hacks or court reporters, but of proper law reporters, a different beast altogether. These are lawyers employed by legal service providers, who also attend court and report proceedings. In contrast with journalists, however, law reporters are only interested in reporting law and procedure, for online and hard copy law reports rather than newspapers, journals or magazines. They, therefore, are the source of public information about how the law develops. Their role does not overlap or detract from that of the journalists. Their readers are all lawyers or similar professionals, but that is unsurprising and unobjectionable. Law is, after all, a learned profession and it is only professionals who are in a position properly to understand most developments in precedent (which is not to say that no legal rulings are ever appropriately reported and discussed by the press and public, just that the majority of the output of the courts of record will inevitably only be read by lawyers).

I am pleased to be able to report that law reporters are in no danger of diminishing. I am less pleased to have to reiterate that this does not detract from the concerns of Mr Banks about the plight of court reporters.

32. A deadly secret

New Zealand, like the United Kingdom, has a fairly comprehensive national health system, although the system does not share the same name and is in some respects perhaps not as comprehensive. Being a far smaller community the opportunities and resources for medical specialisation are necessarily fewer, for example. Nevertheless, it has long been the expectation of New Zealanders that they will receive health care on the basis of need, not ability to pay. Any identifiable exceptions to that rule over the years have always generated strident public debate.

So it was in the mid-1980s, when the government decided it would no longer pay for heart transplants in New Zealand hospitals. Instead, grants would be made available for patients to have the operations performed in Australia. To say that the measure was controversial would be an understatement. It certainly would have come as a painful shock to one Mr Tucker, a patient on the transplant waiting list at the time.

Worse was to follow for Mr Tucker. The grant subsequently offered by the government was nowhere near enough to pay for the necessary treatment in Sydney. Sympathetic newspapers picked up his plight and a national fundraising campaign was held. The campaign appeared to be successful and he travelled to Australia to await his operation.

In the meantime, however, the rumour mill had been fed some grist. It turned out that Mr Tucker had an unsavoury past, having served time in jail for indecent assault. Unsurprisingly, public sympathy for his plight started to evaporate, along with some of the promised funds for his operation.

With his life now imperilled, both by the lack of funds for the operation and the extra stress brought on by the

Published in the *New Law Journal*, vol 162, 28 September 2012, p 1230.

adverse publicity, Mr Tucker applied to the High Court for an injunction restraining further publication of his past convictions. One of the bases of his claim was a purported tort of invasion of privacy. At the time such a cause of action was a novelty in New Zealand law, and indeed in most of the common law world. Mr Tucker therefore had to argue that the New Zealand courts should effectively invent a new tort. He pointed to the United States, where the cause of action was well established.

Leaving aside the legal novelty of his claim, the action was doomed from the start, for one simple reason: the information was already in the public domain by the time Mr Tucker reached the courthouse. Thus, even though the judge expressed some support for the notion of a right to privacy, and asked for "legislative action on some comprehensive basis determining the extent of the right to privacy and the relationship of that right to freedom of speech", Mr Tucker lost his case (see *Tucker v News Media Ownership* [1986] 2 NZLR 716).

Not long afterwards the English courts were to follow the same sort of reasoning in the *Spycatcher* litigation, and it remains the law today: no injunction will be granted, however justified in theory, if it can have no practical effect. This is an eminently sensible principle: there is no point in a court barking at the moon. Any otherwise deserving claimant will have to make do with damages. In Mr Tucker's case, though, that would not have been an adequate remedy in the light of testimony from his surgeon that his heart could not withstand the stress brought on by the publicity.

Suppose, however, that Mr Tucker had brought the application before anyone had discovered the fact of his convictions. Should the court have allowed his application?

At least three reasons suggest he should have lost. First, convictions are a matter of public record, which is as it should be. There is no place for secret justice in a free and open society. Secondly, publishing criminal records might be necessary for public safety, especially when the crimes are sexual offences, as with Mr Tucker's. Thirdly, any interference with the freedom of the press has to be permitted only with the greatest caution.

Moreover, Mr Tucker's crimes rightly induce nausea. It is not difficult to understand why those who had offered money decided that they would rather give it to a different cause once they discovered his past. There is after all no limit to the number of potential worthy causes and the next in line, as it were, would doubtless have been very grateful for the money originally promised to Mr Tucker.

And yet there is something to be said in the other direction. Mr Tucker had been released from prison some years before needing the heart operation, and had not reoffended, so can therefore fairly be said to have been rehabilitated. He had a young daughter who had no knowledge of the convictions and who had endured much stress herself because of his precarious health. She, of course, did not deserve to suffer whatever her father's crimes, though a cynic would say all the more reason for him not to have committed any in the first place.

There is also a point of more general application. If one accepts that health care should be free at the point of need and universally available, as far as resources can stretch, then by definition one does not allow or deny treatment depending on the moral probity of the patient. Society has a duty to treat them all and indeed the Hippocratic oath requires it.

Further, one could say that Mr Tucker had paid his dues and should not be punished twice. The criminal law required that he serve a term of imprisonment – which he had – and nothing else. It certainly did not stipulate that he would be off the list for critical medical care in years to come.

And yet against all that is the fact that Mr Tucker was seeking voluntary assistance from the public. The government had already decided what it was going to provide in the circumstances, and its provision had nothing to do with Mr Tucker's criminal record (we are entitled to assume). The majority of the public would, I suspect, demand the right to know personal details of those seeking its goodwill when picking and choosing who should receive it.

I must admit to wavering back and forth on the issue. Ultimately, I have concluded that the requirement of open justice means that past convictions should not be expunged and thus should remain a matter of public record. Facts such as Mr Tucker's must be rare and should not trump an important principle of general application. In his particular circumstances the answer lay with the state, which could have remedied the situation with an increased grant, rather than suppressing something which the press had the right to publish and the public had a right to know.

The law reports do not record Mr Tucker's subsequent fate. But they do show that an actionable right to privacy was taken up by later judges in New Zealand and elsewhere, although it was some time coming after Mr Tucker's case, as we will now see.

33. Zombies in the High Court

Peter Jackson is New Zealand's best known and most successful film director. His *Lord of the Rings* trilogy won 17 of the 30 Academy Awards for which it was nominated. His first 'mainstream' film, *Heavenly Creatures,* dealt in a sensitive and imaginative fashion with one of New Zealand's most notorious crimes, the Parker-Hulme murder of 1954. He produced the intelligent science fiction film *District 9* and also directed a well-received remake of *King Kong*.

With all that in mind it usually comes as a surprise for people to learn that two of his first three films were "splatter horrors" belonging in the same category as the likes of *Toxic Avenger, Reanimator* and the like. If anything Jackson's films – the superbly named *Bad Taste* and *Brain Dead* – were even more farcical in nature and extreme in violence, albeit very silly violence. I imagine that the target audience for both films was in the nature of drunken students, rather than, for example, senior judges. Yet *Brain Dead* became the subject of a lawsuit, necessitating its viewing in full in the solemn surrounds of the High Court, presided over by the patrician figure of Justice Gallen. It then found its way into the law reports by way of an important ruling for New Zealand law on the issue of privacy (*Bradley v Wingnut Films Ltd* [1993] 1 NZLR 415).

The scene in *Brain Dead* which led to the litigation was filmed in Karori Cemetery in Wellington. The plot, described by Gallen J in as neutral terms as he could muster, involves a woman becoming a zombie after being bitten by an animal at the zoo. Her son sedates her, to the point where she is declared dead and buried in the aforesaid graveyard. The son, who knows she is still alive, goes to the cemetery at night to disinter her, where he is assaulted by four louts, one of whom is in turn attacked

Shorter version published in the *New Law Journal*, vol 162, 2 November 2012, p 1378.

by the zombiefied mother reaching up through the grave. There was a dispute at the trial over whether the scene of the youth on top involved sexual intercourse with the corpse or simply him being disembowelled. Gallen J dutifully recorded the competing arguments before deciding that he did not need to resolve the point in order to dispose of the case.

The priest who had conducted the funeral and burial scene then joins the fracas, attacking the louts with some cinematic kung-fu moves, though he ends up being impaled on a tombstone. In the time-honoured fashion of the genre, a zombie outbreak then spreads and the film proceeds to a bloody finish involving a house fire and the imaginative use of a lawn mower.

It is not immediately obvious why anyone would watch a splatter horror film and complain about being upset afterwards. It rather reminds me of the time I had a concerned parent ask what legal redress might be available for her having purchased a CD which contained no warning of obscene lyrics. On further questioning it emerged that the CD was by the band *Prodigy* – I therefore gently suggested that the fact that the first track was called "Smack my bitch up" might have been warning enough.

Nevertheless, one viewer of *Brain Dead,* a Mr Bradley, took umbrage at the film because the graveyard scene included prominent footage of his family tombstone. Alerted to its existence by a newspaper article about the film, off he went to his lawyer, and off they both then went to the High Court seeking an injunction restraining the defendant from showing any of the offending footage or still images thereof. In support Mr Bradley, whose family claimed to share his umbrage and outrage, wheeled out an academic from the religious department at the local university. The academic gave evidence explaining that in various religions (including Mr Bradley's Catholicism) tombstones had special spiritual significance.

The difficulty facing Mr Bradley was that he had to find a cause of action on which to base his claim; an injunction could not be granted out of thin air. His first effort was to argue that the film amounted to intentional infliction of emotional distress, a tort the classical formulation of which was found in *Wilkinson v Downton* [1897] 2 KB 57. There were two insurmountable problems. First, the harm was not foreseeable. Secondly, any alleged harm had not been directed at Mr Bradley personally – intentionally or otherwise. The film was meant to be nothing other than escapist entertainment, not a tilt at someone's sacred place or their feelings generally.

The next attempted cause of action was invasion of privacy, and it is in this respect that the case is best known legally. Gallen J reviewed the authorities, including the earlier case of Mr Tucker the benighted heart patient. He held that he was "prepared to accept that such a cause of action forms part of the law of this country".

He then went on to consider the various suggested formulations of the tort, and held that whichever way one looked at it, Mr Bradley was doomed to fail. For example, he stated

> "I do not think that a tombstone in a public cemetery containing information which appears to be directed at the public, can be said to be a private aspect of the plaintiff's life, nor do I think that it is subjected in the film to unwarranted publicity or public disclosure bearing in mind the limited extent to which it appears and the limited significance attached to it."

In that respect it was of some importance that the priest was not impaled on the Bradley tombstone in the relevant scene, and there was no significance to the plot that some of the action took place around the Bradley tombstone as opposed to any other.

Sensibly, Gallen J concluded that if Mr Bradley had succeeded it would have

> "imposed restrictions on freedom of expression which would alter the balance against such freedom more than could be justified."

This places the matter in terms instantly recognisable to modern British lawyers familiar with the European Convention on Human Rights, which would have required any breach of Art 8 alleged by Mr Bradley to be balanced with the filmmakers' right to freedom of expression under Art 10, and (hopefully) would have favoured the latter on similar facts.

Still Mr Bradley and his advisers blazed away. The third cause of action was defamation – not of the occupant of the grave, since one cannot defame the dead, but rather Mr Bradley himself on the ground that the film gave rise to "innuendoes" that Mr Bradley approved of the film and/or was involved in its commissioning. The fourth cause of action was the related tort of malicious falsehood. Gallen J gave both fairly short shrift: the alleged innuendoes could not be substantiated, and, as had already been said in the context of the privacy claim, the tombstone was wholly incidental to the film. It had not been chosen in preference to any other tombstone and no aspect of the film had ever been directed at the Bradleys. For largely similar reasons the still more far-fetched cause of action of negligence was also dismissed.

The sixth and final cause of action was trespass. This also failed, and for a ground which seems to me to have been the crux of the entire case, namely that the tombstone was in a public area. A cemetery is not a private place, and is not owned by the families whose relatives are buried there, despite them paying for the rights to individual graves. It is a public space, and to the extent that access is limited, it is limited either by a church or, as was the case for Karori cemetery, the relevant local authority. Mr Bradley's real complaint should therefore not have been with the defendant for filming the scenes in question where it did, but rather with Wellington City Council for allowing access to the cemetery. As the council was not a party to the proceedings the question never arose in the case.

Had it done so – that is to say, had Mr Bradley tried to sue the Council for allowing filming, then I would hope he would still have failed, irrespective of whatever cause of action his advisers conjured up. The reason relates partly to freedom of expression, but rather more to do with the fact that not every complaint is the law's business. In short, some things are just not worth suing over. Splatter horror films are one example.

It follows that undoubtedly the right result was reached in Bradley's case. The film was thereafter able to be released in unexpurgated form, and went on to enjoy critical and commercial success, helping Mr Jackson towards the mainstream career outlined in the opening paragraph above. Perhaps even Mr Bradley has enjoyed one or two of his subsequent films ...

34. It ain't over till it's over: the trials of Naomi Campbell

Part of the role of a supermodel, one imagines, is the ability to generate headlines, and indeed as the cliché goes there is no such thing as bad publicity.

Naomi Campbell, however, one continues to imagine, might disagree on that last point, on the evidence of the past few years anyway. This year she has found herself in the law courts in the Hague, giving evidence in the trial of the alleged mass murderer Charles Taylor. She has, of course, already found her place in English legal history, through her famous privacy action against the *Daily Mirror*.

The *Mirror* was headed at the time by a young editor by the name of Piers Morgan, fully cognisant of the English tradition of press freedom and freedom of speech, and not shy about asserting it. Nor, one speculates, would Mr Morgan have been reluctant to weigh the increased revenue from the anticipated extra circulation against the likely cost of litigation.

It was Campbell's action, more than any other, which established the existence of an actionable right to privacy (expressed in the House of Lords as a right of action in respect of "misuse of private information" – information in respect of which a person has a "reasonable expectation of privacy"). It remains the leading authority on the cause of action and the principle that the right to a private life under Art 8 of the European Convention on Human Rights and the right to freedom of expression under Art 10 are of equal weight, needing to be balanced according to the facts of each case.

Among the beneficiaries of her pioneering cause of action has been a farrago of footballers, entertainers and other "celebrities". Thus far the most successful in terms

Published in the *New Law Journal*, vol 160, 29 October 2010, p 1500.

of damages awarded has been Max Mosley, famous for his role in international motor racing and indeed for his parentage, both of which added a fair degree of spice to his activities which were the subject of a tabloid sting.

The balancing of the right to privacy and the right to freedom of expression forms one of the key debates in political, moral and legal philosophy. Part of that debate in the English context is the more established cause of action of libel, not without its share of recent controversy. The presence of Lord Neuberger as Master of the Rolls has already signalled a move towards freedom of expression and less in the way of privacy and libel, as shown for example in the withering condemnation by the Court of Appeal of Eady J's judgment in *British Chiropractic Association v Singh* [2010] All ER (D) 08 (Apr). Eady J has also recently stepped down as the head libel judge.

Often one gets the impression that the excessively complex libel and privacy laws together with the usually salacious facts result in the court (and indeed observers of the court) not seeing the wood for the trees. Max Mosley is a case in point. What public interest was there in his antics with prostitutes? No doubt the antics did interest a segment of the public, but that is not the same thing. The point is that, although it was outside his home and outwith his family, it was nonetheless a private sexual encounter. No-one else would agree to cameras in their bedroom without their consent and neither Mosley's occupation nor the accident of his birth should make any difference. Campbell's argument was on similar lines: she was receiving treatment akin to medical treatment, and ordinarily both the fact of one's medical treatment and the content of that treatment itself would be considered private. Celebrities, however, always face a problem if the information is already in the public domain: no court is going to expend resources preventing publication of something already well known.

There were other important rulings in the Campbell litigation. The Court of Appeal considered also s 32 of the Data Protection Act 1998. It was held by the House of Lords in a subsequent hearing that Campbell's lawyers' success fee should be enforced notwithstanding the severity of the costs for the newspaper.

As to the parties involved, it seems as though things have moved on. Photographed together on the red carpet for a charity event in February 2010, Campbell and Morgan have at least put on the pretence of reconciliation.

And yet there remains a bizarre coda to the saga. It is nearly 10 years since the offending article was published, and the proceedings began. We have had full consideration by the domestic courts of the issues arising pursuant to Arts 8 and 10 of the Convention. Strikingly, however, the legal battle isn't yet over. The *Mirror*'s appeal to the European Court of Human Rights remains outstanding. Judgment might appear before the end of this year. Whenever it does, one hopes therefore that the Strasbourg court might also find the time to say something about the right to a fair trial within a reasonable time under Art 6(1).

35. The Prince and the Chinese Takeaway

The Duke of Edinburgh is famous for his less-than-politically-correct remarks. Wincing as they often are, he seems to get away with it because he has otherwise been content to play a silent second fiddle to his spouse, who in turn has almost always studiously observed the requirement of her role to be seen as above the political fray, devoid of any revealed political opinions.

By stark contrast, their eldest offspring, the Prince of Wales, seems rather taken with his own opinions and has rarely been shy about expressing them, whether on modern architecture, the environment or the Human Rights Act. In 2005 his propensity to speak out landed him in some bother when a disloyal subject leaked some of his private journals to the press.

The journals concerned his trip to Hong Kong in 1997, when that particular slice of the rump of the Empire was being handed over to the Chinese in what was inevitably referred to as the Chinese Takeaway.

Prince Charles had been in the habit of writing journals for some decades. They were intended as a private record of his travels and were only circulated to a few friends. According to his staff the journals were "candid and very personal", and Prince Charles viewed them as "both a historical record and a bit of fun ... He would try to make them amusing ..." That presumably explains why the Prince referred to the Chinese dignitaries as "appalling old waxworks".

Here an intriguing question arises, namely what on earth the Chinese thought of him in return? If they had had access to an uncensored internet search engine, one suspects they would have disagreed with many of his expressed opinions on the environment, GM crops

Published in the *New Law Journal*, vol 162, 25 May 2012, p 726.

and the like. They would have found his future role as "Defender of the Faith" (or his preferred "Defender of Faith") at variance with their own atheist state doctrine. On the other hand, his dislike of the Human Rights Act might have been closer in line with their own thinking, albeit for different reasons ...

Following the publication of extracts of the journals in a Sunday newspaper, Prince Charles brought proceedings against the newspaper responsible, alleging, inter alia, breach of confidence.

The primary issue concerned the respective weight to be given to the newspaper's right to freedom of expression under Art 10 of the European Convention on Human Rights as against the Prince's right to confidentiality under Art 8.

Both the High Court and the Court of Appeal upheld the claim (see *HRH Prince of Wales v Associated Newspapers Ltd* [2006] EWCA Civ 1776). At para 68 the Court of Appeal said:

> "the test to be applied when considering whether it is necessary to restrict freedom of expression in order to prevent disclosure of information received in confidence is not simply whether the information is a matter of public interest but whether, in all the circumstances, it is in the public interest that the duty of confidence should be breached ..."

It concluded that:

> "... the significance of the interference with Article 8 rights effected by the Newspaper's publication of information in the Journal outweighed the significance of the interference with Article 10 rights that would have been involved had the Newspaper been prevented from publishing that information."

It further held that even leaving aside the fact that the information had been disclosed in breach of confidence (of which the newspaper was fully aware) Prince Charles had an unanswerable claim for breach of privacy. Adding the breach of confidence tipped the balance overwhelmingly in his favour.

The eminent human rights lawyer Lord Pannick QC was not impressed. He argued (*Times*, 16 January 2007) that the fact that the newspaper had obtained the journals in flagrant breach of confidence by an employee of Prince Charles should have been of little weight.

In this respect I would agree: if there was something of pressing public interest (a classic whistleblowing case, for example) the fact that the newspaper had obtained it by dubious means would not affect the relevance or importance of publication.

Pannick argued that the journals were indeed of public interest, for three reasons: (i) they were not concerned with personal gossip but rather "analysis of a major political event by the person representing the United Kingdom"; (ii) they were written by the future monarch "who makes no secret of his wish to influence political events", and (iii) they threw considerable light on the Prince's policy views. In other words the Prince should have been hoist by his own outspoken petard.

Here I would respectfully disagree. Many public figures keep private journals, and most probably make remarks about people in private that they would rather not have published (Alan Clark seems the exception, in deliberately publishing his). Perhaps one Prime Minister despises another, but is able to suppress those thoughts in public for the sake of international relations; would the public interest unarguably lie in leaking his or her true feelings whilst in office? Watergate tapes are one thing; light-hearted personal diaries another.

The fact that Prince Charles has sometimes overstepped the boundaries of public expression that his mother has so fastidiously observed does not mean that he should not be entitled to record private thoughts, and to have that privacy respected – indeed, there are those who wish he would keep all his thoughts in that fashion and should have every encouragement accordingly.

Afterword

Prince Charles was just one of a number of public figures who followed Naomi Campbell down the legal catwalk. Many a "celebrity" ended up spending large sums of money using up the precious public resource of the courts in order to suppress details of their private lives and misadventures. Matters reached a head in the early 2010s with the advent of the "superinjunction", whereby any information – even the identity of the person seeking the court's assistance – was suppressed.

At the time of writing, the Leveson Inquiry into the press has not concluded, and therefore I will say nothing about it.

I would readily accept that there are occasions in which a right to privacy (over and above traditionally confidential information such as commercial secrets, medical details and the like) is justifiable in principle, despite the erosion of free speech that it necessarily entails. It has to follow that interlocutory remedies to preserve that right are also justifiable – the right to privacy would be meaningless if anyone was free to print something prior to trial.

Moreover, there are circumstances in which justice demands absolute confidentiality, such as where a case concerns an ongoing criminal investigation, or issues of national security, or legitimate protection of commercial interests.

Leaving those aside, however, there is some cause for disquiet with regard to injunctions for private matters. Can it be right that footballers are able to clog up the courts by trying to suppress the fact that in dressing room parlance they have been indulging in one too many away games? The right to freedom of expression and the principle of open justice are fundamental to an open and democratic society. They should not lightly be interfered with. While the extra-marital affairs of celebrities might (and should) be a matter of supreme indifference to anyone not personally involved, it does not follow that the law should intervene to silence the press. At the least the burden should be firmly on the applicant to show why the state should intervene on his or her (usually his) behalf.

I would offer the following observations. First, there should rarely be a right to silence details of personal immorality, still less criminal activity such as drug taking. Scarce public resources such as the courts ought not to be expended on a wealthy few hushing up their own moral misdemeanours, which are the result of their freely chosen actions. Freedom of speech needs jealous guarding, and there will be casualties.

Injunctions suppressing sexual misadventures would not likely occur in the United States, with its robust tradition of free speech under the First Amendment. If President Clinton could not claim privacy to keep his extra-marital activities out of the press, it seems unlikely anyone else would stand much of a chance.

The argument in favour of freedom of speech is all the stronger where the conduct in question involves a breach of trust, such as an employment relationship (as indeed in Clinton's case). Certainly there is an argument that children of the parties should be protected, but I do not think that that should be decisive – the state does not guarantee parental infallibility in all respects. If someone is charged with a criminal offence then they may usually be named in the press, despite any opprobrium their children might receive. Moreover, such a person would be innocent until proven guilty, whereas the footballers caught cheating on their wives were seeking injunctions precisely because they were guilty and thus could not sue for libel.

The second point concerns parliamentary privilege. Under Art 9 of the 1689 Bill of Rights, free speech in Parliament is absolute. That priceless jewel in our Constitutional crown exists as the ultimate protection of parliamentary supremacy and indeed democracy itself. Recently such protection was invoked by John Hemming, a backbench Liberal Democrat MP, in order to reveal the fact that Fred Goodwin, former head of RBS, had obtained an injunction which went as far as to prevent Goodwin from being identified as a "banker". (Various wits on the internet promptly observed that Goodwin's performance did not merit the description in the first place.) It has been suggested that a "hyper injunction" would preclude a member of public telling an MP about the existence of such injunctions in the future, lest the MP then render the injunction worthless by disclosing it under the protection of Art 9.

If that is the case (rather than media misreporting) it would seem clearly wrong. The right to discuss something with an MP in the strictest confidence should be unfettered. If the MP then wrongly discloses anything outside Parliament then, rightly, he or she will face the legal consequences. Within either House, however, the protection of Art 9 is absolute and it is for Parliament itself – and the electorate – to censure an MP who abuses it. The member of the public who disclosed the information should be able to claim the protection of privilege, akin to legal privilege which would apply if he or she had discussed something with a solicitor. Parliamentary Privilege is not confined to actual words spoken in the Houses, but extends to actions that advance or are ancillary to proceedings in the Houses (see eg *Pepper v Hart* [1993] 1 All ER 42 at 67–68), though fortunately not, as was held in the *Chaytor* case discussed in chapter 29, claiming expenses ...

The final point is one which applies to many of the classic debates concerning free speech. To put it bluntly, all of the above discussion may be rendered largely irrelevant by something out of the hands of the courts and Parliament. I refer of course to the internet. The English courts can issue *contra mundum* ("to the world") injunctions, but the reality is that since the law (for present purposes) has no reach beyond these shores, it has become – for better or for worse – very much harder indeed to suppress information than ever before. Someone outside the jurisdiction might publish something on the internet that would then be easily accessible to British citizens. It would still be an offence for a British citizen to download and disseminate the information, but readers will need no elaboration of the reality of such a situation.

The only recourse for the government in those circumstances would be to try and censor internet search engines, in the manner of a few largely non-admirable totalitarian regimes elsewhere. I trust such a step is not likely to occur in this country ...

Part VIII: Sport and the Law

Sport, like every other area of human activity, finds its way into the legal system in a variety of forms. Sportsmen and women use the court system for resolving their disputes, voluntarily or involuntarily, and the criminal justice system superintends sporting conduct.

The first case in this part, *Miller v Jackson*, concerns one of the most celebrated judgments from one of England's most celebrated judges, Lord Denning. Unlike many of his better known cases it is far from moral or legal controversy, and is famous instead for its entertainment value, with Denning making no attempt to hide his love for cricket and his consequent disdain for the killjoy that was Mrs Miller.

The second concerns one of England's most celebrated cricketers, Ian Botham, and his teammate Allan Lamb, squaring off against Pakistan's greatest player Imran Khan. Botham and Allan Lamb both showed extraordinary stoicism facing the ferocious fast bowlers of their day, yet behaved in an absurdly thin-skinned manner by bringing a libel action against Imran.

Perhaps Lamb was egged on by having successfully defended a libel action brought by a former Pakistani player, Safraz Nawaz, a few years earlier. But the case he brought with Botham was an unmitigated disaster. About the only thing they got right was not calling Geoffrey Boycott, who appeared instead as a witness for the defence. *Wisden Cricketers' Almanack* (1997 edition) recorded that Boycott

> "provided a bizarre interlude by arriving jacketless from Lord's, wearing a shirt with a sponsor's name, and brandishing a boot in the witness box to try to make a point unconnected with the case. He was silenced by the judge ..."

Which rather confirms the old rule of thumb about not calling a witness if you don't know what they are going to say ... Interestingly, Mrs Gillick, whom we find elsewhere in the book, made an appearance of sorts in the Court of Appeal in Botham's case, as a failed action she had brought against the BBC was cited as the most recent authority reiterating the classic test for libel.

While the Botham/Lamb libel trial was a depressing episode for the claimants, the Pakistani spot fixing affair of 2011 in which three cricketers were found guilty of "spot fixing" was a far more depressing episode for all of cricket. The very ethos of the game, the essence of the sport – of all sport – requires players at an international level to be giving their all, all of the time. Even an apparently minor transgression such as a deliberate no-ball can be, as I have argued, fatal to the expectation of all concerned that the game is being played as it should.

Moving to the different sport of football, John Terry's case raises two entirely disparate points. The first concerns the desirability of racial and religious hate crime legislation. The second is the limit of self-regulation as a substitute for the general law, including criminal law. Both are substantial subjects, but I hope there is enough in the article at least to identify the key points for debate, as indeed has been the hope with all the cases considered in this book.

Finally we turn to the distasteful affair that was the boxing match between Dereck Chisora and David Haye. Whether one is a fan of boxing or not, the idea that a fight could take place on British soil against the express wishes of the duly authorised British boxing authorities is simply wrong. It would be an affront to the rule of law if it was a different sport, but the fact that unlicensed boxing amounts to a criminal offence renders it worse still. Needless to say, it was hardly the first – and will not be the last – example of inept organisation in boxing.

36. The delight of everyone

Elsewhere in this book (chapter 45) I consider Lord Denning's finest hour as a judge, Here, I am concerned with his finest hour as a legal writer – and arguably as a cultural guardian as well. I refer, of course, to *Miller v Jackson* [1977] 3 All ER 338, a work of literature first and law a somewhat distant second.

The facts begin in the following evocative tones:

"In summer time village cricket is the delight of everyone. Nearly every village has its own cricket field where the young men play and the old men watch. In the village of Lintz in County Durham they have their own ground, where they have played these last 70 years. They tend it well. The wicket area is well rolled and mown. The outfield is kept short. It has a good club-house for the players and seats for the onlookers. The village team play there on Saturdays and Sundays. They belong to a league, competing with the neighbouring villages. On other evenings after work they practice while the light lasts. Yet now after these 70 years a judge of the High Court has ordered that they must not play there any more. He has issued an injunction to stop them. He has done it at the instance of a newcomer who is no lover of cricket. This newcomer has built, or has had built for him, a house on the edge of the cricket ground which four years ago was a field where cattle grazed. The animals did not mind the cricket. But now this adjoining field has been turned into a housing estate. The newcomer bought one of the houses on the edge of the cricket ground. No doubt the open space was a selling point. Now he complains that, when a batsman hits a six, the ball has been known to land in his garden or on or near his house. His wife has got so upset about it that they always go out at weekends. They do not go into the garden when cricket is being played. They say that this is intolerable. So they

Published in the *New Law Journal*, vol 161, 23 September 2011, p 1294.

asked the judge to stop the cricket being played. And the judge, much against his will, has felt that he must order the cricket to be stopped; with the consequences, I suppose, that the Lintz Cricket Club will disappear. The cricket ground will be turned to some other use. I expect for more houses or a factory. The young men will turn to other things instead of cricket. The whole village will be much the poorer. And all this because of a newcomer who has just bought a house there next to the cricket ground.

I must say that I am surprised that the developers of the housing estate were allowed to build the houses so close to the cricket ground. No doubt they wanted to make the most of their site and put up as many houses as they could for their own profit. The planning authorities ought not to have allowed it. The houses ought to have been so sited as not to interfere with the cricket. But the houses have been built and we have to reckon with the consequences.

At the time when the houses were built it was obvious to the people of Lintz that these new houses were built too close to the cricket ground. It was a small ground, and there might be trouble when a batsman hit a ball out of the ground. But there was no trouble in finding purchasers. Some of them may have been cricket enthusiasts. But others were not. In the first three years, 1972, 1973 and 1974, quite a number of balls came over or under the boundary fence and went into the gardens of the houses, and the cricketers went round to get them. Mrs Miller [the second plaintiff] was very annoyed about this."

The judgment continues in the same vein for many more pages of the law reports. No summary or extract can properly do justice to Denning's literary craftsmanship, which ought to be read in full. In short, Mrs Miller refused an offer by the club to pay for any damage that might be caused, and instead brought proceedings seeking a mandatory injunction preventing the matches from continuing. The judge granted the injunction and the cricketers appealed.

In emphatically allowing the appeal, Denning held that it was all the fault of the developer for building the houses too close to the ground, the local authority for granting planning permission for him to do so and the Millers for buying one of the houses; and not at all the fault of the cricketers for continuing to play as they had done for decades.

Denning also rejected a suggestion that the cricketers had been rude when asking for the ball back. Instead he rather acerbically lumped Mrs Miller with that description for refusing to give it.

Looking back it seems clear that justice was done, though pedants might be troubled by some of Denning's logic. He explains that "everyone" delights in cricket, though the case seems to be full of those who don't. The authority was obviously a divided lot. As Denning held, the planning department had failed to do its duty by allowing the building of houses so close to the pitch. At the same time, however, the authority's revenue department took such an interest in proceedings that they nudged everyone's rates up or down depending on who was batting: a reduction was introduced after someone's window was broken, and an increase followed after the club told everyone to try and hit fours rather than sixes a few years later. (One can imagine the windfall the residents would have been in for if Viv Richards or Wayne Larkins had moved to the village, though Mrs Miller would doubtless have preferred to pay higher rates and not have to leave the house so often.)

Denizens of the Inns of Court should note the caveat towards the end of Denning's judgment that his *ratio* did not apply in the garden of Lincoln's Inn, where the "windows and people" (in that order?), rather than any cricketers, were entitled to the law's protection. He distinguished the ruling in *Bolton v Stone* [1951] 1 All ER 1078 that cricket should not be played where it was dangerous to do so, on the robustly logical basis that it was different if the cricketers were there first.

Decades later Lintz cricket club is still going strong, and Denning's judgment remains a favourite amongst law students and cricket buffs. The *ratio* of the case is still good law too, and indeed for more than 30 years it ensured that no-one else tried the Margot Leadbetter antics of Mrs Miller. In 2010, however, according to *Wisden Cricketers' Almanack* (p 1646), there was something of a reprise in the Guildford County Court, where one Mr Burgess made the same mistake of moving next door to a cricket ground and then complaining about balls landing in his garden.

No doubt mindful of Mrs Miller's failure to have the matches shut down *in toto*, Mr Burgess sought the more imaginative remedy of a mandatory injunction requiring the cricketers to erect a 25ft high net to catch the ball. He also updated my sitcom reference by whining that he had been "unfairly made out to be a Victor Meldrew figure."

No details are given in *Wisden* of the judgment itself other than the gratifying news that the case was dismissed. *Wisden* adds however that the cricketers fired a waspish parting shot by suggesting that if one didn't like the sound of a klaxon one shouldn't buy a house next to a fire station.

Quite so, although I wonder if Mr Burgess truly resembled Victor Meldrew, in which case his real complaint was probably the intolerable suspicion that someone, somewhere was having the temerity to enjoy themselves.

37. Just not cricket

To a certain generation of cricketing followers, there was something supremely ironic about Ian Terence Botham becoming a Knight of the Realm. Throughout his playing career he was England's perennial bad boy: an aggressive presence on the field and a bon viveur off it, with a legendary disdain of authority. He also performed substantial works for charity, it should be said, and these were cited as part of the reason for his knighthood.

It is also true that in more recent times he has begun to resemble the not-in-my-day whingers he once despised. Then again, Botham has always been certain he is right about everything, it is just that as a player that made him sound like a rebellious youth, but as a commentator it has made him sound like a Truemanesque curmudgeon. So perhaps it is not Botham who has changed, but rather our perception of him. Or perhaps it is part of the inversion of values that different generations sometimes go through, in the same way that a Master of Fox Hounds was once a pillar of society but is now almost ipso facto a criminal.

One for a somewhat quieter life was Botham's teammate Allan Lamb, a South African who qualified for England by residency during the Apartheid era.

On the pitch both had a formidable opponent in the form of Pakistan's Imran Khan, a genuinely great cricketer and a shrewd leader as well. Imran was no more afraid of controversy than Botham, and if he wasn't as hedonistic off the pitch he certainly attracted tabloid attention with his film-star looks and celebrity marriage to the socialite Jemima Goldsmith (whose father rather waspishly – though somewhat prophetically – remarked that Imran would make "a good first husband").

All three played many matches together. No love was lost in any of them. Relations were undoubtedly

Published in the *New Law Journal*, vol 162, 13 January 2012, p 70.

not helped by Botham's acerbic views on Pakistan as a country and a cricketing side.

Their most acrimonious clash, however, came not on the field but in the rather different forum of the Royal Courts of Justice, when in the mid-1990s Botham and Lamb decided to sue Imran for libel.

The action arose out of reported comments by Imran to the effect that all leading players were involved in ball tampering, along with insinuations, so it was contended, that both Botham and Lamb were racist and, bizarrely, "lower class".

Before trial the Court of Appeal had to rule on whether the ball tampering allegations could be libellous given that Imran had made it clear that he himself did not consider it cheating (see (1996) Times LR, 15 July). The answer was that the statements could still be libellous. That was hardly surprising. If Imran had been talking about a serious actual crime then no-one would have suggested that his opinion prevented a libel from having occurred. The test is not what the speaker intended but whether the impugned statement would "tend to lower the plaintiff in the estimation of right-thinking members of society generally". Most cricketing fans consider ball tampering unacceptable, and would therefore have considered an accusation libellous whether Imran approved of the practice or not.

A number of current and former players gave evidence. It is anyone's guess why someone decided to call Geoff Boycott, as blunt a Yorkshireman as ever lived, who duly went on to amuse the court with his riotous opinions. (Years later Boycott would complain during a court case of his own in France that the proceedings were "all in French", thus missing one of the basic principles of French justice.) Almost as risky a witness was David Gower, who answered questions much as he batted – effortlessly, stylishly and with almost no thought to the consequences.

Botham, on the other hand, was as direct and robust in the witness box as he had been at the crease, snarling at the disputed allegations and taking umbrage at what he considered to have been slights about the state of his marriage.

It was all to no avail. The case failed, Botham having apparently alienated the jury much as he once did opposition cricketing fans. It is fair to say that neither he nor Lamb was a gracious loser. Though they chose not to appeal, they continued to resist the costs for almost a decade, eventually losing again in the High Court on that issue (see [2004] All ER (D) 222 (Nov)).

Not much humility about the affair was on display in the respective players' autobiographies (several autobiographies in Botham's case). Botham has continued to work in the media. Lamb retains a lower profile, though for a time appeared with Botham in a series of television advertisements.

Imran, meanwhile, went on to much more worthy pursuits, fully embroiling himself in the maelstrom of Pakistani domestic politics, his commitment to which he blamed for the breakdown of his marriage. He even earned Botham's admiration by building a cancer hospital in Pakistan. One suspects that alongside his political career, libel actions, tabloid gossip or even his entire cricketing career must seem like small fry.

Relations between English and Pakistani cricketers seem to have improved in recent years. That said, Pakistani cricket has had to endure more allegations of ball tampering, leading to a test match being forfeited; a terrorist outrage on its home soil against the touring Sri Lankans; and endless match-fixing controversies, including criminal convictions for three leading players in England in 2011. Even Beefy Botham's career looks tranquil next to all that.

38. Cricketing convictions

In late 2011, three Pakistani test cricketers, Salman Butt, Mohammad Asif and Mohammad Amir, were convicted of conspiracy to cheat at gambling and conspiracy to accept corrupt payments, arising out of Pakistan's tour of England in 2010. They were sentenced to 30 months', 12 months' and 6 months' imprisonment respectively (Amir having pleaded guilty). Butt has recently filed an appeal against sentence. Regrettably, although it is the first such prosecution in the United Kingdom, only a delusional optimist would assume it will be the last. It therefore falls to be considered whether the sentences were justified.

The convictions arose out of a sting by the *News of the World* newspaper in August 2010. Cricket, being amenable to extensive statistical analysis, perhaps more than any other sport, lends itself to "spot betting". Aside from betting solely on the outcome, any number of bets on the procedure of the game are possible – how many boundaries will be hit during the course of the day; who will be the highest or lowest scorer in each innings; how many extras will be bowled and by whom; and so on – in other words, all the minutiae which fills many pages in *Wisden Cricketers' Almanack* each year and considerable amounts of data on websites such as *Cricinfo* as well.

In turn the endless possibilities make it much easier for the unscrupulous bookmakers to try and rig bets. It would be one thing – and hopefully a very difficult one – to persuade an individual player to throw his wicket, still less an entire team to throw a match. Even if a team could be so persuaded, it would take some considerable effort to throw a match without arousing suspicion. It would be much easier on the other hand to persuade someone not to score a boundary off a particular over in a test, which potentially can run to 450 overs, or to bowl a wide or no-ball off a particular delivery. Such would usually – but not always, as we shall see – be inconsequential.

Published on *Halsbury's Law Exchange,* 14 November 2011.

These possibilities gave rise to the three prosecutions. The *News of the World* filmed a sports agent, Mazhar Majeed, counting bribe money and stating that Asif and Amir (both fast bowlers) would bowl no-balls at specified stages of the Lord's test. In the event both did exactly as Majeed predicted. They were not marginal no balls either: the television commentators expressed bewilderment at the extent to which Amir in particular had overstepped.

No balls are commonplace in cricket, particularly amongst fast bowlers, but the odds against predicting exactly when they will occur would be almost impossibly high. Five hundred and forty balls will be delivered in the course of a normal day's test cricket, and the only credible explanation of both players doing exactly as Majeed said they would is that they were indeed in his pocket.

It followed necessarily that Butt had colluded in the affair, because, as captain, he alone had the power to decide who would bowl and when.

Initially cricket's governing board, the ICC, conducted its own investigation, and went on to impose bans of ten years for Butt (of which five were suspended), seven years for Asif (of which two were suspended) and five years for Amir. The criminal prosecution then followed. (Majeed was also convicted after pleading guilty and received the longest sentence of all, but this article is confined to the cricketers themselves.)

The result of the ICC's ban coupled with the sentences of imprisonment is likely to be the end of Butt's career. At the very least Asif's will be seriously curtailed. Only Amir, aged 19, seems likely to play again.

The question thus arises as to whether the offences justified penalties that are personally and professionally ruinous, along with every other consequence of imprisonment.

The answer has to be a resounding yes, for two reasons. The first is the recent history of corruption in cricket. The second is that despite some differing views, it seems to me unarguable that even the slightest spot fix very seriously undermines the game.

As to the first of those reasons, many cricketing correspondents have enjoyed displaying their historical knowledge by pointing out that cricket's origins as an organised sport in something like its modern form lie in an excuse for gambling (see for example Reverend Pycroft's *The Cricketer's Field*, written in 1851).

Corruption of the sort with which Pycroft was concerned had long died out by 1981 when inveterate horse racing fans Dennis Lillee and Rod Marsh famously induced a frosty atmosphere into an already gloomy Australian dressing room by revealing a successful bet on England at 500-1 odds at Headingly. That was properly seen as an innocent if poorly judged act on the part of the two players.

Modern match fixing and spot fixing began a few years after the surge in interest in cricket on the subcontinent which accompanied India's victory in the limited overs World Cup in 1983. It reached world attention in the early 2000s when the then South African captain, Hanse Cronje, was found to have accepted a string of payments for distorting matches. Two senior Australian cricketers, Shane Warne and Mark Waugh, were also found to have had some contact with a bookmaker in the 1990s – most ill advisedly suppressed at the time by the Australian cricket authorities – although it was not suggested they had agreed to alter matches, only that they provided useful information about conditions and players. But it was clear that the involvement of bookmakers with cricketers could not be dismissed as occasional skullduggery on the subcontinent which the rest of the cricketing world could pretend to ignore.

The ICC's response included an inquiry by a former senior British police officer, Sir Paul Condon, but although the issue drifted from headlines, only the most hopeless optimist would ever have assumed that the problem had gone away. The true extent can of course never be known. But we now have judicial confirmation that it still very much exists. That constitutes the first reason why the courts have to respond with stiff sentences as a deterrent.

The second reason is that even apparently insignificant actions such as a no-ball here and there can have a strong influence on the outcome of a match. Not all have seen it that way: in the immediate aftermath of the match at Lord's, a former President of MCC, Field Marshall Lord Brammall, struggled to see what the fuss was about. On 31 August he wrote to the *Telegraph* in these terms:

> "It was most regrettable that this incident was alleged to have happened in the fourth Test ... Let no one, however, try, as I am afraid some have tried to do, to consider this a significant part of the game itself, impinging on the historical reputation of this test match.
>
> The delivery of the odd obvious no-ball would not and did not change the course of the match or the outcome."

Lord Brammall seems to have forgotten many a famous no-ball of test matches past. To take just one example: in the third test of the 2005 Ashes series, Michael Vaughan was bowled early on by a no-ball; he went on to score 166, the highest score of the match, and thus the fact of Glenn McGrath overstepping on one occasion had considerable significance.

But the point is wider than that. As the judge inferred, if the fact of the Pakistani fixing has not cast a pall over every future international fixture, it will at least cause a question, or suspicion, to be raised every time something extraordinary appears to take place; and a central part of the enjoyment when watching sport is witnessing extraordinary events – the tragic dropped catch, the farcical run-out, the ill-judged moment after a day's solid concentration, and so forth. In those circumstances substantial terms of imprisonment were, rightly, inevitable.

39. John Terry, free speech, sport and the law

England football captain John Terry has been charged over alleged racist comments said to have been made during a Premiership football match in October 2011. The details of the charge, set out in a CPS press release, are:

> "On 23 October 2011 at Loftus Road Stadium, London W12, you used threatening, abusive or insulting words or behaviour, or disorderly behaviour within the hearing or sight of a person likely to be caused harassment, alarm or distress which was racially aggravated in accordance with section 28 of the Crime and Disorder Act 1998 ... [c]ontrary to section 31 (1) (c) of the Crime and Disorder Act 1998."

As the case has not been heard I will say nothing more about its facts. Instead I will offer some observations on two related general issues prompted by the incident. The first concerns another aspect of s 28 of the 1998 Act, not raised in Terry's case. The second concerns the general interplay between sport and the law, and the substitution of self-regulation for the criminal law. Both are large issues with far wider application than Terry's case.

Section 28 provides, so far as material:

> "An offence is racially or religiously aggravated for the purposes of sections 29 to 32 below if—
>
> (a) at the time of committing the offence, or immediately before or after doing so, the offender demonstrates towards the victim of the offence hostility based on the victim's membership (or presumed membership) of a racial or religious group; or
>
> (5) In this section 'religious group' means a group of persons defined by reference to religious belief or lack of religious belief."

Published on *Halsbury's Law Exchange*, 21 December 2011.

It might be suggested that abuse is abuse; and made none the better if it happens not to be directed at someone's race. But human history is full of examples of the most appalling examples of abuse specifically based around race. There is therefore some justification in the context of the public order offence of harassment for special condemnation of abuse directed at someone's race.

The more substantive controversy about s 28 concerns the inclusion of religious grounds on an equal basis with race. Certainly human history is at least as riddled with abuse of religions as it is with abuse of racial groups. Also, one of the world's great religions, Judaism, classifies its adherents on matrilineal grounds, rendering it akin to a race (this is a factor which tied the courts in knots in the well-known Jewish Free School case of *R (on the application of E) v Governing Body of JFS* [2009] UKSC 15, [2009] All ER (D) 163 (Dec)), though nothing is offered here on whether Judaism is a race or religion or both.

The usual distinction offered is that religion is a set of ideas, which one may choose, modify or abandon, whereas one has no choice over one's race. As a result, the right to freedom of speech in the form of the right to discuss, debate and indeed lampoon religion is a fundamental feature of a free society, but the same arguments cannot be applied to discussion of race. (That said, in the United States the right to free speech is valued so strongly that even banning racist hate speech is highly controversial.)

The counter is that for some people their religion is so intimately tied to their personal identity it has an equivalent status to race. This may be true for some, but it is not true for all, and more to the point it also has to be seen in the context of the sort of theocratic oppression found in other countries (and in the history of this country) which is inimical to a free society. Recognising that, and the importance of free speech generally, Parliament came up with the following when introducing the religiously aggravated element of the offence in the Racial and Religious Hatred Act 2006:

"Protection of freedom of expression

Nothing in this Part shall be read or given effect in a way which prohibits or restricts discussion, criticism or expressions of antipathy, dislike, ridicule, insult or abuse of particular religions or the beliefs or practices of their adherents, or of any other belief system or the beliefs or practices of its adherents, or proselytising or urging adherents of a different religion or belief system to cease practising their religion or belief system."

(Section 29J in Sch 3 to the 2006 Act.)

The problem should be immediately apparent. Very little that might be said to be an offence under the religious aspects of s 28 will not be alleged to constitute protected speech under s 29J of Sch 3 to the 2006 Act. Then one has to factor in the right to free expression under Art 10 of the European Convention on Human Rights, though s 28 would likely fall within the state's margin of appreciation.

Much the better option would have been not to have introduced the offence in the first place, and to have left any unjustifiable harassment to the general law. Then, whilst harassment of an individual would have remained illegal, there could have been no attempted prosecution of satirical works of art or literature. Nor could there have been any attempt to suppress general public debate about the role of religion in society. Moreover, having fewer such laws would often work in favour of religious believers who wished to advance controversial opinions based on their faith, such as the late Harry Hammond, to use an example from earlier in the book.

Turning to the second issue, where the divide falls between the right of a sporting body to self-regulation and the application of the general law – including of course criminal law – is another classic grey area. Abusive behaviour on the pitch in the form of harassment of opposition players or the referee is hardly unknown in many sports. Then there are the occasional out-and-out physical assaults: for example, the footballer Roy Keane claimed in his autobiography that he had once deliberately injured the player Alf-Inge Haaland. That sort of conduct would constitute *prima facie* evidence of assault. Either way, self-regulation of sportsmen could hardly be said to encompass a case of a sportsman attacking a spectator, such as Eric Cantona's infamous kung-fu kick (though I cannot resist adding that it gave rise to one of the tabloids' greatest headlines: "The shit hits the fan"), given that the spectator never signed up to the jurisdiction of any sporting body simply by attending a match. (The authorities took the same view and Cantona was prosecuted for assault.)

Even if Keane's actions might be appropriately punished by the football authorities themselves, it is hard to argue why an actual brawl such as the Kevin Tamati/ Greg Dowling encounter known to all antipodean rugby league followers, which took place off the pitch after both had been sent to the sin bin, should not attract the interest of the CPS if public order offences under the 1998 Act do. Admittedly most rugby league players, especially of that era, would have thought it demeaning to refer their disputes to the police, but as the law student favourite of *R v Brown* [1993] 2 All ER 75 held, consent is no defence to an assault occasioning actual bodily harm (though it does seem to be in the case of boxing ...).

Next one might consider actions such as blatantly faking a penalty. A player might be disciplined for doing so, but would that be adequate punishment – let alone sufficient redress for the opposition – if it altered the result of the match (say it was an extra time penalty in a knock-out competition) with huge financial consequences?

It follows that the dividing line between self-regulation by sporting bodies and the general law is somewhat less than logical or principled. I will leave it to readers to ponder what a principled approach might be.

Afterword

On 13 July 2012 John Terry was acquitted. However, Terry received disciplinary sanctions from the Football Association following an investigation by an Independent Regulatory Commission.

40. An ignoble day for the noble art

Recently on *Halsbury's Law Exchange* Simon Hetherington wrote a thoughtful piece on boxing (23 May 2012). He stated candidly at the outset that he was not a boxing fan. For my own part, I would admit to being an inveterate fan of the sport, although I haven't followed it closely for a few years now. Even the most avid boxing fan, however, has to admit that the activity gives rise to serious moral and legal questions. And even if one finds satisfactory answers to those questions in principle, no-one can be happy – from a legal, moral or sporting perspective – with the way in which boxing is run, as the embarrassing saga of the planned fight between David Haye and Dereck Chisora demonstrates.

The first question a lawyer might ask is why boxing is legal at all. Ordinarily, hitting someone with the intention to render them unconscious would amount to a serious criminal offence. The immediate riposte is that boxing is done by consent. But consent is usually no defence to a serious criminal offence, as the law student favourite of *R v Brown* [1993] 2 All ER 75 demonstrates. In that case the House of Lords found that the fact that the defendants had consented to sado-masochistic sexual activities was no defence to charges of unlawful and malicious wounding, and assault occasioning actual bodily harm (offences under ss 20 and 47 of the Offences against the Person Act 1861 respectively). Their reasoning was that public policy required that society be protected by criminal sanctions against a cult of violence which contained the danger of the proselytisation and corruption of young men and the potential for the infliction of serious injury.

Is there a moral difference between damaging genitals for sexual gratification on the one hand, and

Published on *Halsbury's Law Exchange*, 7 June 2012.

damaging brains for sporting enjoyment, money and the entertainment of spectators on the other? If there is, it is not obvious. Of course, other activities (smoking or drinking for a start) and indeed other contact sports involve a risk to one's health. But only in boxing (or the various forms of full contact martial arts, which incidentally are usually regulated even more badly than boxing) is damaging another person's health the whole point of the activity rather than a risky side effect.

R v Brown was and remains a controversial decision, and one reached by a bare majority. For what it is worth, I think it was wrongly decided, and it would be interesting if someone challenged it pursuant to the European Convention on Human Rights, presumably with reference to the right to private life guaranteed by Art 8. But the case remains good law at least for now, and it is hard to square the underlying principle with the continuing legitimacy of boxing.

We therefore start with the fact that boxing is a moral and legal anomaly. How has it survived in an age of health and safety? I suggest there are four main reasons: first, because it has the veneer of respectability conferred by the fact that it is a regulated activity; secondly, because it has been sanitised in the public eye by the Queensbury rules; thirdly, because of its history and tradition, which means there has been little public call for its abolition (though centuries of history and tradition did not save fox hunting); and fourthly, the natural resistance, particularly in England, to state paternalism – if people box voluntarily and with knowledge of the risks involved, most consider that it is not the state's business to stop them.

A side note should be made about the Queensbury rules. They were not the first attempt at boxing rules (for example, in 1743 a set of rules known as the London Prize Ring Rules were published), but they were the reason why boxing took on its modern form, with a fixed number of rounds for each bout, restricted target areas and forms of striking, and compulsory gloves. Ironically these were only partially successful. Although the number of potential injuries must have been reduced by the restrictions on possible forms of hitting, it is generally held that the use of gloves has actually increased the risk of death or serious injury. This is because in bare knuckle fights contestants would damage their hands quite quickly, especially with head punches, which thereafter limited the effectiveness of their blows (and thus explains why fights would last for dozens of rounds). Conversely, with gloves hand injuries are rare, even over 12-round fights, meaning punches can be thrown with maximum force throughout. While gloves cushion blows they do not reduce their force; the same brain injury will occur even if superficial injuries such as cuts are reduced. Thus the Queensbury Rules are a good example of the law of unintended consequences.

Another side note should be made about the boxing associations. These act as the sanctioning bodies and award titles in each weight division. There are now any number of competing associations, whose proliferation has led to a sometimes comical devaluation of the concept of "world champion". Many boxing fans will have never even heard of some of the fighters and some will not have even heard of all the *soi-disant* authorities. So too with weight divisions: once upon a time there were only three ("heavyweight" started at ten stone ...) which was manifestly too few; nowadays there are manifestly too many.

Of greater legal interest, however, are the licensing authorities. In Britain the chief authority is the British Boxing Board of Control (BBBC). Theoretically, only fights under the auspices of a recognised authority are lawful, although there are exceptions: the authorities seem to turn a blind eye to some forms of bare knuckle fights, for example, whilst two people who put on gloves and spar in an unlicensed gym are not likely to attract a prosecution either.

But let us return to licensing authorities and the gaping regulatory hole which Simon Hetherington identifies. His article was prompted by the forthcoming fight between Haye and Chisora. The fight is not being sanctioned by the BBBC. Nevertheless it is taking place in Britain, apparently legally, because it is being sanctioned by another board, that of Luxembourg. Can it be right, Mr Hetherington asks, that one country's authority can license a fight in another country, particularly when that other country's authority has explicitly refused to sanction it?

One thinks immediately of the tragic end to the greatest of all boxing greatest careers, that of Muhammad Ali. By 1981 he was a washed up has-been, a shadow of his former self, yet continued to rage against the dying of his sporting light, like so many boxers before and since. He wanted to fight the journeyman Trevor Berbick. No regulatory authority in America would have anything to do with it. But the shameless Bahamian boxing authorities did sanction the fight, which went ahead and was, as everyone predicted, an horrific spectacle as the once-great Ali was hammered by the younger Berbick. To add to the disgrace the Bahamian organisers were so inept that no stopwatch or bell had been officially provided: a watch had to be borrowed and then someone improvised with a cowbell.

That "contest" was bad enough as an instance of greed above all else. But imagine how much worse – indeed, absurd – it would have been if the fight had been held in America under the auspices of a foreign authority, against the wishes of the duly constituted American authorities? That is the scenario that is threatening to occur with the Haye/Chisora fight.

Admittedly Haye against Chisora does not have the feel of an imminent disaster in the way that Ali against Berbick did; both fighters are presumed competent. But it has only come about because someone has managed to persuade the Luxemborg authority (which has no professional fighters under its jurisdiction) to license the fight and a German company to promote it – on British soil. The British board does not want the fight to happen. Its reasons are not the point – if one disagrees with them, then one should appeal, or apply to challenge the decision by way of judicial review. One certainly should not have the option simply to rope in some other licensing authority to circumvent the inconvenience of one's own regulator.

If boxing is to have any credibility as a sport, let alone as an activity forming a glaring exception to the criminal law, then it has to be conducted in a respectable fashion. It does no one any credit or respect to be able to dodge the appropriate British regulatory authority on British soil with a small country's equivalent organisation. It would be embarrassing in other sports, if one could find one in which it would happen. But in boxing it should also be illegal – not simply unlawful, but as illegal as organising a criminal activity, which, after all, is precisely what unregulated boxing amounts to.

According to recent press reports, the European Boxing Union has threatened Luxembourg with expulsion for licensing the fight. Let us hope it is prepared to carry through with that threat, and that the whole tawdry affair is thereby brought to a swift and appropriate conclusion.

Afterword

The fight did indeed take place, on 14 July 2012. Haye won by stoppage in the fifth round.

Part IX: Crime in Our Time

Criminal law is the one area of law that consistently attracts public interest. I think there are two broad reasons why. The first, obviously enough, is the lurid subject matter. The second is the rather more worthy reason that criminal law is a powerful manifestation of the values of any particular society. What actions or omissions any particular society deems criminal; how it chooses to try those suspected of offences; and the conditions and duration of punishment of those it convicts all say a very great deal about that society.

Elsewhere in the book I have written in praise of the British judicial system in the civil law context. That applies also with respect to the criminal law, certainly on a comparative basis. There are very few countries in the world – and have been very few throughout recorded history – in which I would rather stand trial for criminal charges than the United Kingdom in the present day.

Having said that, no-one would pretend the present system is perfect, or anything close: it is always underfunded, sentences are inconsistent between different classes of offending (for example, why are deaths caused by dangerous driving rarely treated as seriously as murder or manslaughter?), prisons are overcrowded and re-offending rates are high. Perhaps it is time for a radical rethink of the punishment regime at least.

The first case considered in this part, *R (on the application of Rusbridger and another) v Attorney General* [2003] 3 All ER 784, shows what happens if old statutes are left on the books as some sort of quaint historical memorabilia. It is all very well for pub quiz questions, but the danger is that someone might take one of the statutes seriously.

The last two cases were high profile events in 2011: the Joanna Yeates murder and the behaviour of the press, and the appropriate sentences for the August rioters.

The Yeates murder press presented exactly the same problem as the Fatty Arbuckle trial of Part II: irresponsible tabloids cashing in on public interest and taking advantage of freedom of speech to the detriment of a fair trial.

Finally, the August rioters raised the issue of appropriate sentences or, as I have argued, appropriately long sentences.

41. Looking for trouble

From time to time cases bring up old laws that have been languishing on the books for years without anyone noticing. By the 1950s, for example, the Court of Chivalry had not sat for two centuries, and most assumed it had ceased to exist. Yet it was revived in the celebrated case of *Manchester Corporation v Manchester Palace of Varieties Ltd* [1955] 1 All ER 387: since no case or legislation could be found which had formally abolished the court, it had to be extant.

An earlier and more dramatic example might be *Ashford v Thornton* (1818) 106 ER 149, where the defendant in a murder case managed to escape liability by invoking the ancient right of trial by battle. As with the *Manchester Palace* case, the right (to the mode of trial) had not been explicitly abolished by Parliament, and the court accordingly had no option but to rule that it was still available. The plaintiff, a slight chap unwilling to try his luck, declined to join battle, and so the defendant effectively escaped a murder charge.

More recently, as discussed earlier in the book, Helen Duncan found herself prosecuted under an eighteenth century statute with "witchcraft" in the title.

It was perhaps with an eye to such instances that early in the twenty-first century the *Guardian* newspaper set out to generate a few headlines for itself, which ended up with the case of *R (on the application of Rusbridger and another) v Attorney General* [2003] 3 All ER 784.

The *Guardian*'s editorial line has long favoured Britain becoming a republic. In late 2000 its editor, Alan Rusbridger, wished to publish a series of articles calling for a peaceful abolition of the monarchy.

Presumably Mr Rusbridger regretted Britain missing out on the European revolutions of two centuries earlier. Back in those turbulent days Westminster was not unaware of events taking place across the channel, and its responses included the Treason Felony Act 1848. Section 3 of that Act provided, so far as material:

> "If any person whatsoever shall, within the United Kingdom or without, compass, imagine, invent, devise, or intend to deprive or depose our Most Gracious Lady the Queen ... and such compassings, imaginations, inventions, devices, or intentions, or any of them, shall express, utter, or declare, *by publishing any printing or writing,* . . . or by any overt act or deed, every person so offending shall be guilty of felony ..." (emphasis added)

Lord Steyn painted its historical backdrop in these terms:

> "1848 was the year of revolutions on continental Europe, but there was only one Chartist demonstration on 10 April 1848 in a relatively tranquil Britain. But there was a fear that the contagion of revolution, with its associations with the Terror after 1789, might spread to Britain. This was probably one of the reasons why Parliament passed the Treason Felony Act 1848. A further factor was that while the Treason Act 1351 applied to the whole United Kingdom it was unclear whether later statutes (such as the Treason Act 1795) extended to Ireland. Certainly Parliament was told that this was the principal mischief to be addressed. There was another objective. The Treason Statute of 1351 was still in place as it is in part to this day. The Treason Act 1795 was passed to facilitate the prosecution of constructive treasons: it did so by criminalising them as treasons. But juries were reluctant to convict defendants of what were sometimes perceived to be political charges but carrying the death penalty. The 1848 Act therefore provided that certain constructive treasons were to be felonies, punishable by life imprisonment. It did, however, specifically provide that conduct penalised by the 1848 Act could still be charged as treason."

A few prosecutions had followed the Act's inception (see for example *R v Mitchel* (1848) St Tr (NS) 599 and *R v Duffy* (1848) St Tr (NS) 915), but none had taken place since 1883. Nevertheless, Mr Rusbridger was concerned that s 3 would technically be broken by the articles he intended to run. He received legal advice that the interpretation of s 3 of the 1848 Act would be "read down" under s 3 of the Human Rights Act 1998, on the ground that s 3 of the earlier Act was incompatible with Art 10 of the European Convention on Human Rights.

Ostensibly to allay his fears, Mr Rusbridger proceeded to engage in correspondence with the Attorney General, seeking to have the advice he had received about the interpretation of the 1848 Act confirmed by way of a declaration, and to be assured that he would not be prosecuted. The Attorney General declined to grant any declarations but, to no-one's surprise, did not bring a prosecution either.

Dissatisfied, the *Guardian* went to court seeking (i) a declaration that two decisions allegedly taken by the Attorney General during his exchange of correspondence with Mr Rusbridger were erroneous in law; (ii) a declaration that s 3 of the 1848 Act, when read in the light of the Human Rights Act, did not apply to persons who evinced in print or in writing an intent to depose the monarch unless their intent was to achieve that by acts of force, constraint or other unlawful means; and alternatively (iii) a declaration of incompatibility of s 3 of the 1848 Act with the Human Rights Act.

The Divisional Court gave the application short shrift. Adopting the same approach as in the assisted suicide cases, it stated that it was not appropriate for declarations as to the criminality or otherwise of conduct to be made, save in exceptional circumstances, and certainly not before the conduct itself had occurred. The rest of the claim was disposed of in equally summary terms.

The Court of Appeal had slightly more time for the *Guardian*'s campaign, holding that the newspaper should be allowed to proceed with both the claim for a declaration on the proper construction of s 3 of the 1848 Act and the alternative claim for a declaration of incompatibility. The Attorney General appealed to the House of Lords.

Giving the leading judgment, Lord Steyn set out the historical background in the passage quoted above. He held that the case might indeed fall within the exceptional category justifying a declaration about non-prosecution. When he arrived at the key question of what order should be made, however, he allocated all of one paragraph:

> "The part of section 3 of the 1848 Act which appears to criminalise the advocacy of republicanism is a relic of a bygone age and does not fit into the fabric of our modern legal system. The idea that section 3 could survive scrutiny under the Human Rights Act is unreal. The fears of the editor of The Guardian were more than a trifle alarmist. In my view the courts ought not to be troubled further with this unnecessary litigation."

The rest of the House agreed and so the *Guardian*'s application was dismissed. It was ordered to pay the costs of the appeal as well.

Mr Rusbridger did not become the editor of a national newspaper for nothing, however, and managed to fashion the following victory cry (note the strange use of lower case):

> "Although the attorney general has won this appeal, we are delighted that the House of Lords' ruling unanimously vindicates the Guardian's position: that this anachronistic law is incompatible with the Human Rights Act and should be repealed by parliament.
>
> ...
>
> If the attorney general had made a statement of the obvious two years ago, the litigation would not have been necessary."

It is true that all of the Law Lords had rubbished s 3 of the 1848 Act. Mr Rusbridger's last paragraph, however, argues that the litigation had been "necessary" because of the obstinacy of the Attorney General. That was not the view of the House of Lords at all – as we have seen, Lord Steyn's parting remark was precisely to the opposite effect. Moreover, Lord Scott had this to say about the *Guardian*'s expressed fears:

> "My Lords, I do not believe a word of it. It is plain as a pike staff to the [*Guardian*] and everyone else that no one who advocates the peaceful abolition of the monarchy

> and its replacement by a republican form of government is at any risk of prosecution."

He went on:

> "[T]he valuable time of the courts should be spent on real issues. I have already expressed my non-belief in the reality of the [*Guardian*'s] alleged fear of prosecution. I repeat it. I do not suppose there is any school debating society that has not regularly debated the issue of monarchy versus republic. Everyone who reads newspapers or magazines will have read numerous articles and letters extolling the advantages of a republic over a monarchy and advocating a change — and vice versa, of course. These articles and letters have not led to prosecution or any threat of it. Nor have those responsible for school debating societies received visits from the Special Branch. This has been the state of affairs throughout my adult life but it is, I do not doubt, of longer standing than that. There has been no prosecution under the Act since 1883. The enactment and coming into force of the Human Rights Act 1998 made the tolerance de facto of advocacy of peaceful political change a tolerance de jure."

It was, he concluded, unnecessary litigation seeking to obtain obvious results.

The case provides an example of how common sense can override the strict letter of the law, and that the survival of some arcane nonsense on the statute book can indeed be overlooked. In that respect it provides justification for the Attorney General having the discretion whether or not to bring a prosecution, though as the case also reiterated, that discretion does not equate to a right to change the law by a blanket policy of non-prosecution.

Parliament should have found time to expunge the offending part of s 3 of the 1848 Act. Then again, it probably had better things to be doing – as indeed the House of Lords thought it did as well.

42. When the press oppress

Two principles fundamental to English law are open justice and freedom of the press. The right of the public to know via the press who has been charged with what is one of the key features that distinguishes a free society from the sort of tyrannies where those deemed not to be on message politically disappear and are never heard from again.

Equally fundamental, however, is the right to a fair trial, which requires among other things that an accused is judged solely according to the evidence before the court, not the fevered imaginings of the more populist elements of the press. Balancing the competing principles formed the basis of the recent case of *HM Attorney General v MGN Ltd and another* [2011] All ER (D) 06 (Aug).

The proceedings arose from the murder of the student Joanna Yeates in Bristol in late 2010. Miss Yeates' body was discovered on Christmas Day, a few days after she had been reported missing. She was found to have been strangled. On 30 December, her landlord, one Christopher Jeffries, was arrested on suspicion of her murder.

Once there was a suspect the tabloids wanted information – sensational if possible – and went looking for it. On 31 December, the *Daily Mirror* splashed across its front page: "Arrest landlord spied on flat couple"; "Friend in jail for paedophile crimes"; and "Cops now probe 36-years old murder" (a reference to an unsolved murder in the same area in 1974). Inside the paper further insinuations in the same sort of florid prose were made about Mr Jeffries' behaviour and the earlier murder. It also called him a "nutty professor" with a "bizarre past" who was known as the "local oddball". The following day it repeated most of those points and added more detail about the apparent similarities between Miss Yeates' death and the 1974 murder.

Published in *Criminal Law & Justice Weekly*, vol 175, 17 September 2011, p 591.

On the same day the *Sun* newspaper got in on the act as well. It took the time to tell its readers that Mr Jeffries was "obsessed by death" and that he scared children accordingly. It claimed that he was obsessed with blonde women (Miss Yeates was blonde as it happened). It then offered a series of observations by people who had known him, all of which were along the lines that he was eccentric and slightly disturbing.

Subsequently, however, another individual admitted responsibility for killing Miss Yeates and was charged accordingly. Mr Jeffries was therefore set free and entirely exonerated. The Attorney General began proceedings against the publishers of the *Daily Mirror* and the *Sun* for contempt of court. The contention was that by their articles ranting about Mr Jeffries being a disturbing freak they would have imperilled his chances of a fair trial, if the proceedings against him had ever reached that stage.

By s 2(2) of the Contempt of Court Act 1981, it was necessary for the prosecution to prove to the criminal standard that each publication created "a substantial risk that the course of justice in the proceedings in question will be seriously impeded or prejudiced". The risk had to be assessed as at the date of publication and had to be in respect of extant proceedings. Thus it made no difference that, shortly after the articles, Mr Jeffries was exonerated and would never face trial. Further, the case against each defendant had to be considered separately.

The publishers placed reliance on the observations of Sedley LJ in *Attorney General v Guardian Newspapers Ltd* [1999] EMLR 905 that, if an appeal by the defendant on the ground of prejudice would not succeed, the publishers should not be guilty of contempt.

The court described that authority as having "wholly evaporated" in the light of subsequent cases such as *Attorney General v Associated Newspapers Ltd* [2011] EMLR 17, where Moses LJ stated that the law of contempt was concerned with preventing a publication because of the risk of serious prejudice, whereas an appeal would be concerned whether there had been such prejudice as rendered the conviction unsafe. The fact that no actual prejudice resulted from the publication could not prevent it from being a contempt within the meaning of s 2(2), although no doubt the lack of actual prejudice would be a relevant factor in considering whether the offence under s 2(2) was made out.

A point arose concerning the right of freedom of expression under Art 10 of the European Convention on Human Rights, and its interrelationship with the right to a fair trial guaranteed by Art 6. Their lordships gave it short shrift: any interference with the Art 10 rights of the publishers depended on proof to the criminal standard that the publications in question had created a substantial risk of serious impediment or prejudice to the course of justice. That fell comfortably within the limitations to Art 10 acknowledged in the Convention itself.

The court described the material in the *Daily Mirror* publications as "extreme": although the paper had not positively asserted that Mr Jeffries was guilty of paedophilia or the 1974 murder, substantial risks were created to the course of the trial. Had Mr Jeffries ever faced trial, he would have had a serious argument that a fair trial was not possible. That argument would probably have failed, but it would have been properly made, and would have resulted in extra court time and costs accordingly. Moreover, witnesses might have been reluctant to come forward in the light of the vilification of Mr Jeffries, or could have had second thoughts about what they had intended to say about him. The offence was therefore made out.

The *Sun* articles were not as grave but nonetheless would still have risked damaging Mr Jeffries' defence preparation, and therefore also constituted contempt.

As well as giving the last rites for Sedley LJ's formulation of the test for contempt, as set out above, five points of general interest emerge from the case. First, the requirements of s 2(2) stand in marked contrast to submissions sometimes made at trial or on appeal that a fair trial is not possible because of the publicity. Under the latter, the court has to assess the totality of media coverage, whether before or after any arrest, whereas under s 2(2) only the individual publication is to be considered. Change has been mooted to align the two tests but nothing has come to pass.

Of course one newspaper is not responsible for what another prints. But any story will be affected by the context of what is already known about the subject. If suspicion about a person has already been raised it will presumably affect the way readers approach a subsequent story; and it is not expecting too much of one media outlet to expect it to be aware of what stories others have already run.

The second point concerns the question of whether s 2 should remain confined to extant proceedings, rather than anything printed before an arrest has been made. On the one hand, it might be said that a newspaper article should not attract a criminal prosecution because of events that happen after it is published, even though it may come to be relevant in considering whether the trial can actually proceed.

On the other hand, as the court pointed out, the rule might lead to inconsistent outcomes. In the Yeates murder, the individual who was ultimately charged did not dispute responsibility and therefore Mr Jeffries dropped out of the picture. Imagine, however, that A, a wholly innocent man, is vilified by the press but not ultimately charged. B is charged at a later date and denies responsibility. His denial axiomatically carries the accusation that someone else is responsible. The opprobrium heaped upon A may well divert attention at the trial of B, who will seek to exploit suspicion that the press wrongly raised. Since, however, the proceedings against B were not "active" at the time the publicity was directed against A, no contempt would have been committed.

It is true that A would have an action in libel, so the restriction on s 2 does not afford the press carte blanche in respect of pre-arrest publications, but A might be indigent or otherwise unable or unwilling to sue. I would therefore agree that the matter should receive legislative consideration.

Thirdly, one wonders why the newspapers printed such ill-advised articles in the first place. Rumour has it that in-house counsel are fewer on the ground in Fleet Street nowadays, presumably as a result of cost-cutting. If that is true then, regrettably, more legal transgressions can be expected.

Fourthly, it is surprising that the judgment did not consider the effect of the internet. One of the central planks of the publishers' defence was that the articles would have faded from the jurors' memories by the time of the trial. But the articles would still have been readily obtainable online, and may have been towards the top of any internet search, which would necessarily find the most recent first.

The internet also gives rise to the fifth and final point: no prosecution will be possible in the case of articles published overseas, although they may be readily accessible to British citizens. For the same reason I always suspected that "superinjunctions" for privacy would be a flash in the pan, since anyone minded to do so could expose material the subject of an injunction with impunity if they were based outside the jurisdiction. It can only be hoped that the fair trial process is not destroyed in that fashion. For all of the arguments in favour of free speech, one can find many instances of tabloid journalism grossly interfering with justice. One thinks of Hollywood circuses from the Fatty Arbuckle scandal of the 1920s to the OJ Simpson fiasco of more recent times (see chapter 4): few would wish to see justice conducted – and corrupted – in the same manner in this country.

43. Sentencing rioters

Riots in London are nothing particularly new. A sermon by one Dr Sacheverell in 1709 preaching the doctrine of non-resistance found him on trial for impeachment, because taken to its logical conclusion it would have rendered the Glorious Revolution unlawful, and the Whig government of the day was not having that. In response Sacheverell's supporters rioted throughout the Square Mile – in support of the man who preached obedience to the law. In more recent times riots occurred in the early 1980s due to racial tensions and later in the same decade in response to the "poll tax". In August 2011, however, riots broke out which were not due to some ironic political feelings, nor police treatment of minority citizens and a general feeling of racial disharmony, nor an objection to what was seen as an unfair tax. Instead, the abiding images were of people nonchalantly wandering through clothing and electronics shops to acquire what they would otherwise have to pay for, or "shopping with violence" as it became known. Libraries and bookshops on the other hand remained untouched; one chain of the latter offering that it might be a positive thing if someone stole from it, though no one did in the event.

In an article in *Criminal Law & Justice Weekly* ([2011], vol 175, p 596) Caron Thatcher and Emmanouela Mylonaki of London South Bank University considered the sentences handed out following the 2011 riots. The theme of their article was that some of the sentences were disproportionately high, at least in the case of offences not involving violence. It seems to me, however, that there are indeed reasons particular to riots which do justify higher sentences than ordinary incidents of public disorder or theft.

Moreover, one suspects the August 2011 unrest will not be the last of its kind. It certainly was not the first of its

Shorter version published in *Criminal Law & Justice Weekly*, vol 175, 3 December 2011, p 721.

kind, even if, as mentioned, the motivation of the August rioters did not seem to have very much in common with that of dissidents from ages past.

One independent point should be dealt with first. The authors report the chair of a magistrates' court claiming that the court had received "a government directive" that anyone involved in the rioting should receive a custodial sentence. Similar sentiments were reported elsewhere in the media at the time. If any such "directive" had emanated from the executive it would have been thoroughly improper, and should have been disregarded accordingly. It is fundamental – and legally trite – that the executive should have no say over the prosecutorial process. Indeed the first ever Labour government was brought down after it tried to interfere with the Attorney General's independence (in what became known as the *Campbell* case of 1924). For precisely the same reasons the executive should have no influence over the judicial process.

It is worth restating the principle despite the apparent obviousness because unfortunately the previous administration did not always observe it. As was reported in the journal *Justice of the Peace* at the time (169 JPN (5 March 2005) 168 and 173 JPN (2 Apr 2005) 248), neither the Labour government itself nor the Attorney General of the day behaved constitutionally over the Hunting Act and the challenges thereto in the mid-2000s. The present government should at least aim to do better.

Back to the August rioters. In any high-profile case it is of obvious importance that the rule of law applies and the court is not swayed simply by the unpopularity of the offender or offenders before it. Instead the usual rules of sentencing have to be applied. The general principles, as set out by Ms Thatcher and Ms Mylonaki, are codified in s 142(1) of the Criminal Justice Act 2003. These are the familiar punishment, deterrence, reform and rehabilitation of offenders, protection of the public and the making of reparation by offenders to victims.

In gauging the seriousness of any offence, the court is required to consider the offender's culpability, together with any harm which the offence caused, was intended to cause or might foreseeably have caused (s 143(1)).

How should these principles be applied to rioters? Taking advantage of the police being overstretched would not tell in an offender's favour, though it might be a mitigating factor if one could argue that an offender was normally a law abiding person who acted spontaneously, rather than a career criminal.

As against that, deterrence is a legitimate sentencing objective, as reflected by s 142(1), and discouraging the public from starting civil unrest or taking advantage of it for criminal purposes is a factor not ordinarily present in theft cases. On that basis longer sentences for rioters would indeed be justified.

Furthermore, retribution is not wholly irrelevant to sentencing. If someone has blatantly and wilfully transgressed the rules of society in the cynical fashion of those opportunistically helping themselves through a broken shop window, then society ought to have the right to respond as the application of a moral principle; it should not be viewed as crude revenge.

One other issue to which riots of any nature give rise is the cost and other resources associated with a sudden increase in the number of offenders. It will always be tempting for more lenient sentences to be passed, and a greater proportion to be non-custodial, simply on the basis that the country is struggling to accommodate prisoners as it is. At least in theory such issues should have no impact on the process of the courts: it is for the executive to find the necessary resources, and a properly convicted offender should not have a windfall just because the state has been inefficient in responding to the situation.

In these austere times, however, one wonders just how much apparently fundamental aspects of the criminal process – from public funding of defence counsel through to appropriate prison terms; and the conditions in prisons themselves – will be degraded or abandoned altogether. That remains to be seen.

Part X: Public and Private Battles: Civil Cases

This final part consists of several cases from the most common sort of litigation – that between private parties.

The first, *Wilson v Racher*, concerns one of the milestones in employment law in the (gradual) transformation from what Edmund Davies LJ called a "Czar-serf" relationship to the modern concept of "mutual respect". Mutual respect was not, however, much in evidence in the case itself, as the language of Wilson the disgruntled gardener indicates ... Moreover, for all of Edmund Davies' modern sentiments, the phrase "master and servant" still appears in the judgment ...

There follows another classic judgment by Lord Denning, who remains one of the best-known judges in English history. Denning was responsible for many judgments which were controversial both legally and morally. His dislike of the desiccated black letter law championed by Viscount Symons might be said to be the antithesis of what made England a desirable location for commercial lawyers – namely, its championing of certainty. Yet his innovation of the Mareva injunction was one of the most important developments in modern commercial law and it is impossible to imagine doing without it.

The remaining cases were chosen because each contained an interesting moral or logical puzzle. The two cases about vintage Bentleys, for example, raised an issue which must arise almost every day in the world of antiques and vintage cars – namely, what constitutes originality? Is the *Last Supper* still Leonardo's painting, when it is almost all restoration (Leonardo having not listened to the experts on how to create frescoes)? Frank Lloyd Wright in a similar fashion specifically rejected the advice of structural engineers and concrete experts when designing *Fallingwater*. Since then the house has had to be rebuilt considerably to address the very problems that Wright was warned about; it is therefore exactly what he wanted it not to be. So, despite looking almost identical, and having had a continuous physical presence in the same place with the same name, is it still the original house?

I have to confess though that it was the factual background to the Bentley cases – the halcyon days of motor racing, when WO's finest, or *le camion plus vite du monde*, squared off against Ettore Bugatti's more elegant creations – that inspired me to research and write the article.

On a similar note, it was my youthful obsession with heavy metal bands that led me to the Judas Priest litigation. Of all the cases in this book, it has to be the most farcical, consisting as it did of allegations about "subliminal messages" in the band's records encouraging suicide. That was preposterous. For a start, "subliminal messages" have about the same scientific basis as astrology or homeopathy. Even leaving that aside, there weren't any subliminal messages in the Priest songs to begin with. Even leaving that aside, the alleged statement the subject of a subliminal message ("Do it") did not mean anything in context because it had no context.

Next we have the case of a man jumping out of the window to escape police custody, then suing the police for the injuries he suffered on landing. I am relieved to say he lost, but not without a very senior judge – Sedley LJ – holding otherwise. The reason his case was felled was the old Latin maxim *ex turpi causa non oritur actio*, which means that "no man may profit from his own wrong".

The same maxim arose in a very different context in the final case considered in the book, that of *Stone & Rolls*. The case involved a particularly knotty question about whether auditors should be liable for negligence in not identifying their clients' crooked scheme, something regrettably more topical by the day. The case is a classic example of the ordinary application of sound rules leading to an arguably unsound result, and as such is an interesting conundrum on which to finish the consideration of cases in this book. The article is followed by a short afterword with a few thoughts drawing together some of the common themes seen over the cases, and where the common law might go next.

44. The disgruntled gardener

Tolethorpe Hall in Little Casterton, Rutland, is a fine example of an English country house and grounds. The gentle Gwash river meanders past the house, with the picturesque Gwash valley behind. It is hard to think of a more classically English rural scene.

Despite the tranquil setting, the estate has seen its share of human drama over the years. It was for a time the seat of the Browne family, one of whom (Robert, c. 1550 – c. 1633) lead the "Brownists", who campaigned for a congregational form of organisation for the Church of England before being run out of the country. In the early 1970s, a few centuries after Browne, and nearly a millennium after the first record of a house on the site, the estate found its way into the law reports by way of a landmark employment dispute.

At the time the estate was owned by one Mr Racher. The head gardener was a Mr Wilson (no relation). The two failed to get on from the start, and the disgruntled Racher went looking for a way to rid himself of Wilson.

In June 1972 he thought he saw his chance, when Wilson stopped work on a Friday afternoon because of rain. On the Sunday afternoon, Racher was in the garden with his wife and their three young children when Wilson passed and greeted them. That friendly salutation was as good as things got. Edmund Davies LJ later described what happened next:

> "Thereafter the defendant (Racher) showered the plaintiff (Wilson) with questions. He shouted at him, and he was very aggressive. He accused the plaintiff of leaving his work prematurely on the Friday afternoon. The plaintiff explained that he had stopped cutting the hedge only because it would have been dangerous to continue, whereupon the defendant said, 'I am not bothered about you, Wilson, that's your lookout' ... when the defendant

Published in the *New Law Journal*, vol 162, 12 October 2012, p 1294.

> accused the plaintiff of shirking his work on the Friday afternoon, there is no doubt that the plaintiff used most regrettable language ... 'If you remember it was pissing with rain on Friday. Do you expect me to get fucking wet?'"

Racher promptly purported to sack Wilson for using inappropriate language. Wilson countered by bringing proceedings for wrongful dismissal.

No doubt Racher would have been encouraged by the earlier *Pepper v Webb* [1961] I WLR 514, where another argumentative gardener had been held justly dismissed following his declaration that "I couldn't care less about your bloody greenhouse or your sodding garden".

The difference was that in Pepper's case the court found that the gardener's statement had constituted a clear refusal to undertake his duties, and also that the remark had come after a course of conduct in which the gardener's work had been generally unsatisfactory. Racher, on the other hand, had conceded that Wilson was a competent gardener. He was therefore stuck with the inappropriate language as his only defence. He lost at first instance and appealed to the Court of Appeal.

Edmund Davies LJ, giving the lead judgment, set out the facts as above and went on to discuss the authorities. Here he signalled that change was due:

> "Many of the decisions which are customarily cited in these cases date from the last century and may be wholly out of accord with the current social conditions. What would today be regarded as almost an attitude of Czar-serf, which is to be found in some of the older cases where a dismissed employee failed to recover damages, would, I venture to think, be decided differently today. We have by now come to realise that a contract of service imposes upon the parties a duty of mutual respect."

He went on to conclude that the Wilson/Racher contretemps was all rather unfortunate, but at the same time all of Racher's own making. Wilson's language might have been distasteful (though there had been no finding that the children had heard it) but Racher's unreasonableness was worse. The appeal was therefore dismissed.

The case has long been superseded by a surfeit of legislation and regulation in the employment sphere. Much of the latter derives from European Directives, a development few foresaw back in 1972 despite Britain's accession to the EEC that year. Yet the case is still mentioned in legal literature as a milestone in the transformation of the conceptual framework of employment law from sanitised serfdom to mutual respect, as discussed by Edmund Davies LJ.

I wonder what Racher thought of it all. History suggests the case might have been the least of his worries: although I can find no trace of his subsequent life, the estate was sold off just a few years later. It was acquired in 1977 by the Rutland Theatre of the Stamford Shakespeare Company, by which time the house had apparently fallen into a derelict condition.

The Shakesperean company, by contrast with the estate's previous incumbents, is still flourishing today. Accordingly, instead of Wilson's salty language, the house and grounds must now regularly echo to insults along the lines of "Thou Mammering Folly-Fallen Pumpion", "Thou Saucy Flap-Mouthed Dewberry" and "Thou Lumpish Toad-Spotted Gudgeon".

Robert Browne of the Brownists, as a contemporary of the Bard, might have been more *au fait* with the language, and would have noted the reference to his movement in Twelfth Night, but I imagine Wilson the gardener would have appreciated the sentiment behind the insults more ...

45. "... the greatest piece of judicial law reform in my time ..."

Lord Denning is perhaps the most famous twentieth-century English judge. His fame derives from several sources: partly from the number of high-profile cases on which he sat; partly from his preference for justice as he saw it over precedent; and partly due to his inquiry into the Profumo affair, which, he later recalled, produced his one and only best seller. (It was also known as the "raciest Blue Book ever", though presumably not in the face of much competition.)

Perhaps uniquely amongst common law judges, Denning is also famous because of his judgment writing style. It certainly endeared him to generations of law students, though not all law teachers: a curmudgeonly sort at my *alma mater* used to sneer at Denning's "short sentences and simplistic reasoning".

Still, Denning's judgments could never be accused of lacking clarity, and his unarguably short sentences could be crafted with such skill that his judgments on occasion attained the status of works of literature, as any reader of *Miller v Jackson* [1977] 3 All ER 338 will attest.

Born in 1899, and a veteran of the Great War, Denning displayed the values of his generation more than once, but he could also be forward-looking, perhaps most notably when ruling on the right of a deserted wife to remain in the matrimonial home. His judgments in the fields of property and contract were less well known publicly, but equally controversial in the legal profession: another professor of mine once suggested Denning "never met a plaintiff he didn't like" (presumably Mrs Miller excepted).

Somewhat surprisingly, however, what Denning called "the greatest piece of judicial law reform in

Published in the *New Law Journal*, vol 161, 17 June 2011, p 854.

my time" did not arise from casting off the patriarchal shackles of outdated social mores. It did not even concern substantive law. Instead, it was the creation of the pre-trial remedy of the Mareva injunction, by which assets in the jurisdiction can be frozen before trial in order to prevent unscrupulous defendants from removing them and thereby rendering any litigation fruitless: *Mareva Compania Naviera SA v International Bulkcarriers SA* [1975] 2 Lloyd's Rep 509.

The origins of the remedy are found in *Nippon Yusen Kaisha v Karageorgis and anor* [1975] 3 All ER 282, a case heard a month before *Mareva*.

Recently Lord Neuberger complained, with some justification, about the length of modern judgments. He would certainly have had a point in comparison with the *Nippon Yusen Kaisha* case – the lead judgment was all of four paragraphs long. Denning observed that it

> "has never been the practice of the English courts to seize assets of a defendant in advance of judgment, or to restrain the disposal of them. ... We know, of course, that the practice on the continent of Europe is different."

He then opined that it was time to revise that practice, and went on to grant the order, pointing out that if the defendants had grounds to object they could always apply to discharge it.

It was considered afterwards that the judgment might be defective, since the court had not been referred to *Lister v Stubbs* [1886–90] All ER Rep 797, where it had been stated that there was no jurisdiction to grant such an injunction. Thus, on 23 June 1975, Mareva Compania Naviera SA applied for similar relief to Nippon Yusen Kaisha, and addressed the *Lister v Stubbs* point directly.

On the later occasion the judgment ran to all of three pages. Denning dealt with the *Lister* point breezily. He referred to s 45 of the Supreme Court of Judicature (Consolidation) Act 1925, which provided that an injunction could be granted "in all cases in which it shall appear to the Court to be just or convenient ...", and pointed out that its predecessor section had been given a very wide interpretation in *Beddow v Beddow* (1878) 9 Ch D 89. As it was just and reasonable to grant the injunction, Denning did so.

Roskill LJ agreed that the remedy was justified. As to the legal novelty, he pointed out that the charterers could always apply to the court to discharge the injunction, and referred almost sheepishly to the terms of the charter as providing a means of distinguishing *Lister v Stubbs* "if necessary". Ormrod LJ concurred but declined to write a separate judgment as the application was *ex parte* (ie the other side had not had notice of the hearing and did not take part in it).

It has to be said that the grounds for distinguishing *Lister* seem rather shaky. But the commercial justifications were unanswerable, and the point was never appealed further. Instead Mareva injunctions became standard practice, and a few years later Parliament codified the practice in the Supreme Court Act 1981. The jurisdiction was subsequently extended to include orders of worldwide application, and even cases where there is no substantive claim in England. Renamed "freezing order" in the form of newspeak introduced by the Civil Procedure Rules, the remedy continues to form a substantial part of the business of the Commercial Court.

Denning, aged 75 at the time, took advantage of the absence of any mandatory retirement date and continued to sit until the early 1980s. He died in March 1999 aged 100.

Counsel for Mareva, Bernard Rix, is now Rix LJ and a resident of Denning's old haunt of the Court of Appeal. One imagines that the number of times he has had occasion to recall that day in June 1975 over the course of a long and distinguished career in commercial litigation must be very considerable indeed.

Afterword

There was insufficient space in the original article to mention some of Denning's more controversial statements, such as his views on the Guildford Four or on multicultural juries. A comment on the latter led to his resignation in the early 1980s and is often cited, along with his views on trade unions, as evidence that Denning perhaps was not such a liberal champion after all.

Nor was there space to mention some of the entertaining correspondence he received from aggrieved members of the public after his controversial changes to family law (one letter railed against him for letting the chaps down by allowing irritating ex-wives to have a claim on the matrimonial home, and asked Denning politely but firmly to do everyone a favour and drive his Rolls (it should have been Royce) off Beachy Head). But the *Mareva* case and the case of *Miller v Jackson* discussed in the section on Sport and the Law hopefully give some flavour of the Denning phenomenon and an insight into Denning's continuing, if slightly diminished, popularity amongst lawyers and particularly law students.

46. Old number one or new?

A favourite talking point of sporting hacks is the so-called "golden age" of any particular sport. For cricketing writers it is usually a few decades before they were born. For boxing writers it is probably the era when there were actually fewer belts than boxers to compete for them. Rugby union for its part will always have a divide between fans of the amateur and professional eras respectively.

As for motor racing, the favourite period for the cognoscenti seems to be the interwar years. That was when motor racing took on a serious, organised flavour rather than the rudimentary beginnings of the pre-Great War Gordon Bennett Cup, although the cars remained the product of men in sheds wielding spanners rather than robots in factories.

One wonders, incidentally, what modern health and safety mandarins might have made of driving in excess of 100 mph in vehicles with no seat belts or roll cages, and with suspension that may as well have been derived from a skateboard …

One of the celebrated marques of the age was Bentley, winner of Le Mans in 1924 and every year from 1927 to 1930. Bentley's success was due in no small part to its drivers, the celebrated "Bentley Boys", known for an equal taste for Dionysian excess and physical danger.

Chief amongst them was Captain Woolf Barnato, heir to a diamond fortune and an extraordinary all-round sportsman. For both the 1929 and 1930 Le Mans race the winning entry was Barnato's Speed Six model which came to be known as "Old Number One". Tragically the car crashed at a race in 1932, killing its driver, Clive Dunfree.

It was that crash that substantially led to the car's disputed provenance: the bodywork was ripped off but the mechanics survived. A new body with the old radiator

Published in the *New Law Journal*, vol 176, 24 February 2012, p 302.

was added, and thereafter Barnato used it as a road tourer before selling it in 1939. Thereafter it passed through several sets of hands until, at the end of the 1980s, it was acquired by Bentley enthusiast Edward Hubbard.

Hubbard agreed to sell it to a company, Middlebridge Scimitar Ltd, for £10m, but the sale fell through after the company formed the view that the vehicle did not deserve the title of Old Number One, being no more than a replica. Hubbard issued proceedings to enforce the contract. The case was heard before Otton J.

The *dramatis personae* included two extraordinary witnesses. The first was Wally Hassan, by then aged 85, who had been Barnato's chief mechanic all those years ago.

The second was Barnato's daughter, Diana Barnato-Walker MBE. Born in 1918, she had known the Bentley boys as a child and well recalled her father's fondness for Old Number One. Like Hassan she made a ringing impression on Otton J, and that was without him recording any of her independent achievements. Those included ferrying Spitfires during the war as an "ATA girl" and becoming the first British woman to break the sound barrier. Back on the ground she became a Master of Fox Hounds.

Both supported the plaintiff's case adamantly, despite in Hassan's case having made a few contrary remarks in a ghosted autobiography some years ago. Hassan, giving an insight into the more rigid class system of the day, stressed that he always tried to reuse existing parts, "to save my guv'nor money".

The case turned on an interesting philosophical issue: was the car deservedly called Old Number One when there was nothing physical left of the car from before the crash in 1932? If not, at what point did it change? When 50% had been replaced, assuming that that could be measured? Should those parts one would expect to replace, such as spark plugs, be considered differently from less perishable parts such as the bodywork?

An analogous example might be HMS *Victory*. Almost all her planks have been replaced at some point, but she has been continuously moored at Portsmouth for 200 years, and at no point has she undergone a comprehensive reworking or rebuilding, nor has she been decommissioned. She has simply had an organic replacement of parts as and when required, and to suggest she no longer deserves her name would seem illogical. At the least it would be hard to identify the point at which she changed from being original to replica.

On the other hand, consider the Punch cartoon of a cricket bat, said to be 12 years' old and having "had two new blades and three new handles." One would have a hard sell to pass it off as the original.

During the course of the trial, a three-stage test was postulated: (i) historical continuity; (ii) physical originality; and (iii) owner's intent. The car in question passed the first and third, though on any view failed the second. That was not necessarily fatal, however, rather on the same basis as the *Victory*.

Otton J went on to rule in the plaintiff's favour, having regard to the logbook, the Bentley service records, the Bentley Drivers' Club register, the witness evidence and the application of the three-stage test. One important point was that there was no car with any competing claim to be Old Number One: only that belonging to Hubbard had the requisite provenance.

It is necessarily a grey area, but ultimately I would respectfully agree with Otton J. Old Number One was originally a racing car, after all, and thus one would expect continuous changes to be made, including repairs after any crashes. Perhaps its value would decrease if few or no original parts remained, but that is a different matter from whether it deserves the name at all.

47. What's in a name? Another vintage Bentley case

No sooner had the previous article been written than I had the pleasant surprise of reading about another mechanical survivor from the blood and thunder days of the Bentley Boys. Once again the question of originality arose in the context of litigation over a classic Bentley whose purchaser alleged it was not the car they had thought it to be.

The case was brought by the ironically named Mercedes Brewer against the well-known vintage Bentley dealer Stanley Mann, his company and a finance company. Mrs Brewer, with the finance company's help, paid £425,000 for a 1930 "Speed Six" model sold by Mr Mann.

After a year's happy motoring Mrs Mann suddenly stopped paying the hire purchase instalments. She contacted an auction house, who said that the car was unworthy of the description "Speed Six", because that applied to a particular type of engine which had only been added to her car during a later restoration. Meanwhile, the finance company had repossessed the car and sold it back to Mr Mann for the same price as Mrs Brewer had paid. Mr Mann then restored it further and sold it on for some £675,000.

At that point, one might have assumed, there would be no dispute – Mrs Brewer had disposed of the car, the finance company had got its money back and Mr Mann had made a profit. Yet the first two were still unhappy: Mrs Brewer felt she had been misled, while the finance company had incurred costs of about £61,000 in recovering and storing the car before Mr Mann bought it back. Mrs Brewer was first out of the blocks issuing proceedings.

Her action was founded in collateral warranty: she asserted that there had been an oral warranty that the Bentley was a genuine 1930 Speed Six containing an

Published in the *New Law Journal*, vol 176, 6 & 13 April 2012, p 510.

authentic engine. Mr Mann admitted describing the car as a Speed Six, but argued that that had been a statement of opinion, rather than a contractual warranty. He further argued that he had made no warranty about the engine other than that it had been "prepared to Speed Six specification", and that any contract had been with his company not himself.

The claim against the finance company was founded on the hire purchase contract, which Mrs Brewer contended had been breached by the car failing to comply with description. The company denied liability and counterclaimed for the £61,000 mentioned above.

Somewhat surprisingly, the judge, Anthony Thornton QC, found for Mrs Brewer on all points argued – and some that had not been. Most unsurprisingly the defendants appealed.

The Court of Appeal dismantled the judgment piece by piece. It severely criticised the judge for attempting to rewrite his judgment after it had been handed down, and for unjustly questioning Mr Mann's honesty – something that had not even been in issue in the case. It felled the case against the finance company (and upheld its counterclaim) with a single blow – the company had not misdescribed anything.

No doubt it all made most uncomfortable reading for the judge, but of more general interest was whether the car had merited the description of "Speed Six" irrespective of what Mr Mann had actually said. The issue was not quite the same as with the Old Number One litigation (which the Court of Appeal thought had in fact over-influenced the judge), because the earlier case had turned on whether the vehicle was a known individual car, rather than one of a type. Here the dispute concerned whether the car happened to be one example of the 177 Speed Sixes produced, which Mrs Brewer argued depended on an original engine.

Mr Mann on the other hand argued that all that was necessary to be an original Speed Six was for the car to contain some part of the original chassis with the original chassis number stamped on it. That was also the view of the Bentley Drivers Club and (unsurprisingly) Mr Mann's expert witness. Anything beyond that, he argued, was a matter of opinion.

It should be noted that almost all surviving cars from the era would have undergone significant modification and restoration, particularly racing cars, which might be altered from race to race. Moreover, in those days it was common for cars to have their bodywork built by a specialist coachbuilder, entirely separate from the chassis and engine (indeed, Mrs Brewer's was one such example). Interestingly it was the maker of the latter two components that was considered to be the manufacturer.

The Court of Appeal sensibly held that an authentic and continuous documentary history was not the same thing as an item's description. A vintage Bentley that had been rebuilt out of a piece of the chassis with the number stamped on it would still be worthy of its name. Thereafter the market value would reflect how much was original and what sort of provenance the vehicle had, but that was a different issue from whether it would merit the description at all.

Unhappily much of the litigation in Mrs Brewer's case did not make comparable sense. The fact it was brought at all was nonsensical given the costs involved. Worse, the matter will still have to go back to the High Court for a retrial on certain remaining issues unless the parties settle. I doubt they need reminding that the money expended thus far could probably have bought several other Bentleys instead.

48. (Not) Breaking the law

Much of my youth was mis-spent listening to heavy metal bands from the 1970s and 80s. Since then I have found it amusing watching the genre go from being called a prime factor behind the decline of Western Civilisation to its saviour.

The redemption has come from a realisation that the bands, or the better ones at least, were actually proper musicians who played according to traditional methods, as opposed to manufactured pop or the sort of unmusical noise which finds favour amongst my teenage neighbours. And yet it was once a common contention that all the imagery around swords, sorcery, devils and the undead one finds throughout the heavy metal canon constituted unmitigated evil, or at the very least was not suitable for children.

In 1990 that argument reached its zenith – or nadir – when the veteran British band Judas Priest were sued in the United States by the parents of one James Vance. The action followed an attempted double suicide by Vance and his friend Raymond Belknap. Belknap died but Vance survived with serious injuries (though he died three years later). Both had consumed marijuana and alcohol immediately prior to the incident, and had generally led troubled lives for many years. Despite that history Vance's parents formed the view that the suicide attempt had resulted from the pair listening to the Priest album *Stained Class*. They issued proceedings against the band seeking damages accordingly.

The first hurdle that the plaintiffs faced was the robust protection of freedom of expression provided in the US by the First Amendment to the Constitution. The strategy they adopted was to argue that there had been "subliminal messages" on the album, which should not qualify for First Amendment protection because the recipient

Published in the *New Law Journal*, vol 161, 15 July 2011, p 994.

would be unaware of them: there would be no exchange of information or other functioning of the marketplace of ideas, nor expression of personal autonomy, nor any of the other principles of free speech as understood in American jurisprudence. At a preliminary hearing, that argument was accepted – not without some controversy – and the case proceeded to trial.

The plaintiffs' burden remained formidable nevertheless. They had to establish that the band had deliberately placed a message on the record, which was inaudible (but still identifiable) and thus "subliminal", and that the message had a direct, causative link to the suicide attempts.

The band members, who can be forgiven for not taking the writ entirely seriously initially, attended trial in a solemn manner, with their usual S&M-looking garb replaced by sober suits, offset slightly by the expansive hairstyles common to all metal bands of the time. They denied that any subliminal messages had been placed on the album. It was pointed out that any number of apparent phrases could be "heard" by playing the record – or any other record – backwards, and that most such "phrases" were as innocent as they were nonsensical.

The particular message alleged to be present by the plaintiffs was "do it", which immediately raised the unanswered question "do what?" The band remarked that if they had been going to insert any such message, it would have been along the lines of "buy seven copies of this album" and not a commercially detrimental injunction for fans to kill themselves.

The judge ultimately held that the claim failed due to lack of causation: the tragic actions of Vance and Belknap could compellingly be ascribed to other factors.

Justice was therefore done, although the judge's prior holdings remain disquieting. They include the statement

> "the 'Do It's' on the record were subliminal because they were only discernible after their location had been identified and after the sounds were isolated and amplified".

But, as one of the defence witnesses subsequently wrote (Dr T. Moore, "Scientific Consensus and Expert Testimony: Lessons from the Judas Priest Trial", *The Skeptical Inquirer*, vol 20.6, Nov/Dec 1996), something not consciously discernible is not necessarily unconsciously discernible either.

Dr Moore also pointed out that there is "no evidence whatsoever that subliminal directives can compel compliance".

By allowing the case to proceed to trial, rather than dismissing it summarily, the judge allowed the junk science on which the plaintiffs' assertions were based to gain the veneer of plausibility, or at the least the oxygen of publicity. The proceedings also left the band incurring significant and unrecoverable legal costs.

The plaintiffs' lawyers were just as much to blame for advising their clients to bring an absurd case. They may as well have fashioned an ecclesiastical action on an image of Christ seen on a piece of chapati bread.

Predictably the publicity had some effect. Fellow British metal legend Ozzy Osborne also found himself sued in America over his record *Suicide Solution*, but the case failed because there were no detectable subliminal messages and the overt exhortations in the lyrics qualified for First Amendment protection.

Attention was granted to the INXS song *Suicide Blonde*, but the tune was exculpated because it referred to hair colour - somewhat ironic in view of Michael Hutchence's subsequent death. Presumably, however, radio stations stopped playing the Billie Holiday classic *Gloomy Sunday* or the theme to M*A*S*H (*Suicide is Painless*) around the same time.

With original recordings now almost exclusively in the digital format one hopes we might now be spared "analysis" of supposedly hidden messages in tape distortion, feedback or "white noise". But I suppose that would be to underestimate the human imagination ...

49. A lack of common sense

One popular urban myth tells of some wit in America (it is almost always America, for some reason) who allegedly claimed under an insurance policy that 24 of his expensive Cuban cigars had been destroyed in a "series of small fires". After the insurers refused the claim he sued and won, so the myth goes on, because the wording of the policy was ambiguous. But he was then promptly arrested and charged with arson.

There are two problems with the story. First, every insurance policy ever written has excluded intentional damage by the insured. Secondly, you cannot be convicted of arson for destroying your own property. Nevertheless the myth has been so popular – and apparently convincing to the lay person – that I have seen it reproduced as fact in an otherwise respectable national newspaper.

I suspect the newspaper was taken in because editors and their readers rather enjoy stories about the legal system apparently acting directly contrary to basic common sense. Sadly not all examples are fictitious, as a case from the early 2000s, *Vellino v Chief Constable of Greater Manchester* [2001] EWCA Civ 1249, will illustrate.

In the early 1990s Mr Vellino was well known to the police and something of a folk hero in his local community. He lived in a second floor flat and was frequently arrested there. Often he would try and escape by jumping out of the window. In September 1994, he was arrested as per usual at the flat. Almost immediately he broke free and employed his customary escape route. This time, to his misfortune, he landed badly and suffered severe injuries including a fractured skull, brain damage and tetraplegia. He brought proceedings against the police alleging that they had stood idly by as he was making his escape, in breach of the duty of care that they had owed him once he had been arrested.

Essentially his argument was that the police should have saved him from himself: they would have known he would make a run for it; that he would jump out the window; and that there was a serious risk that he would cause himself substantial harm thereby.

The judge framed the issues in this manner:

> "Analytically there are two different questions, was there a duty of care and, if so, is the defendant prevented from recovering damages by the application of the principle ex turpi causa non oritur actio."

The *ex turpi causa* rule (as it is usually written) translates as "no-one may profit from his own wrong". It arises in many different contexts. The classic example is one thief suing another for his share of the stolen goods. Even if he had a carefully drawn up contract the *ex turpi causa* rule would defeat the claim before it started.

In Vellino's case the defendant police constable relied on the rule to argue that Vellino was trying to break the law, and if he broke himself instead that was his own lookout, even if the police were somehow to blame for not stopping him.

The judge held that there was no duty of care on the police to begin with to save Vellino the villain from himself, and therefore the *ex turpi causa* rule did not need to be considered.

If he had found the police liable, the judge would have apportioned blame so that Vellino bore two-thirds of the responsibility and his damages would be reduced accordingly. Vellino appealed.

In the Court of Appeal Schiemann LJ repeated what he had said in an earlier case, *Sacco v Chief Constable of South Wales Constabulary* [1998] CA Transcript 1382, where the claimant had tried to sue for injuries incurred in escaping from a police van. Schiemann LJ had held, first, that the claimant was guilty of his own misfortune, having done something which he knew or should have known was dangerous. If his judgment was impaired by alcohol that was his own fault too. Secondly, he was engaged in a criminal act, and as a matter of legal policy no-one should be able to recover damages against the police if he hurt himself as part of that illegal enterprise. The basis of such recovery had to be either an allegation of a breach of duty owed to him not to let him escape, or of a duty owed to him to take care that he did not hurt himself if he tries to escape. There was no reason to create such a duty.

Schiemann LJ indicated that he stood by his reasoning in *Sacco*'s case and there was nothing in a recent Law Commission report (The Illegality Defence in Tort (2001) (Law Com no 160)) to change his mind. Vellino's case would therefore fail as well.

Sir Murray Stuart-Smith agreed. His conclusions on the law were (see para [70]):

> "(1) The operation of the principle [*ex turpi causa*] arises where the claimant's claim is founded upon his own criminal or immoral act. The facts which give rise to the claim must be inextricably linked with the criminal activity. It is not sufficient if the criminal activity merely gives occasion for tortious conduct of the defendant. (2) The principle is one of public policy; it is not for the benefit of the defendant. Since if the principle applies, the cause of action does not arise, the defendant's conduct is irrelevant. There is no question of proportionality between the conduct of the claimant and defendant. (3) In the case of criminal conduct this has to be sufficiently serious to merit the application of the principle. Generally speaking a crime punishable with imprisonment could be expected to qualify. If the offence is criminal, but relatively trivial, it is in any event difficult to see how it could be integral to the claim. (4) The [Law Reform (Contributory Negligence) Act 1945] is not applicable where the claimant's action amounts to a common law crime which does not give rise to liability in tort."

All of which seems obvious. As well as the Latin one might add a phrase of more common parlance – "he asked for it".

It is therefore surprising to find a dissenting judgment from Sedley LJ. He pointed out that if police officers (or a fellow criminal) wantonly shot a criminal, they might still be liable for assault despite the *ex turpi causa* doctrine. There should be no distinction in principle between an action for negligence (as in the instant case) and for assault. If the police officers in *Sacco* had left the rear doors of the van open and placed an inebriated person at the back with no restraint, and he had thereby fallen out, it would have been wrong for the police not to be liable in negligence.

He concluded that arresting officers indeed owed prisoners a duty not to afford both a temptation to escape and an opportunity of doing so when there was a known risk that the prisoner would do himself real harm, even if much of the blame for hurting himself would ultimately come to rest on the prisoner himself.

As to Vellino's own stupidity, or (more judicially) criminality, Sedley LJ considered that that would be appropriately reflected when apportioning damages, and agreed with the judge below that Vellino should carry two-thirds of the responsibility. He finished by complaining about the newspaper headlines denigrating the Law Commission report and offering that:

> "to expect a judiciary to modify its decisions as to what the law and justice require because of what it fears the media would make of them is to ask for the surrender of judicial independence".

I am not sure that the view of the public should be entirely irrelevant. Either way, the majority's reasoning seems compelling. Sedley LJ seems to have overanalysed the case, or at the least miscategorised it. It was not a case where the police had actually attacked the claimant. Nor was it analogous to putting a drunken individual in a situation where he was almost bound to be harmed.

Rather, it was a case where the police arrested someone. That person knew full well he was thereafter lawfully required to accompany the police. Instead he made a run for it. That was entirely his own choice, which he made in the knowledge that it was as illegal as it was dangerous (unless he was inebriated, which was also his own choice and equally no excuse).

Unless the police had actively encouraged or compelled him, to permit the claimant to recover damages would have been simply unrealistic, as well as an offence against common sense. The reasoning of Schiemann LJ and Sir Murray Stuart-Smith seems clear, damning and compelling.

50. Laying the blame

At first sight, the case of *Stone & Rolls Ltd (in liquidation) v Moore Stephens (a firm)* [2009] UKHL 39, [2009] 4 All ER 431 seems an unpromising candidate for a book of general interest rather than technical, black letter law. It concerns the liability of an auditor for failing to detect fraud, or, more generally, the question of who should carry the can for the fraud of someone unable to compensate his victims – not normally the stuff of a cause célèbre. But the case also provides a good example of a classic legal dilemma: how to deal with the occasional unreality of otherwise sound legal rules. As such it throws up some nice logical questions. In depressing economic times it is a case that is particularly topical as well.

Mr S was the sole directing mind and will as well as the beneficial owner of Stone & Rolls Ltd (the company). He used it as a vehicle for defrauding banks. By the time that the fraud was discovered, the money had (predictably) vanished.

Both S and the company were sued for deceit by a bank which was the principal victim of the fraud. The bank obtained judgment in its favour but, since the money had been spirited away, neither S nor the company could meet the debt. The company therefore became insolvent.

The liquidator brought proceedings against the company's auditors. He argued that if the auditors had done their job properly then S's fraud would have been discovered earlier and stopped. The auditors applied to strike out the claim. They argued that, even if the breaches alleged had occurred, the action was founded on the company's own fraud and was therefore met by the defence *ex turpi causa non oritur actio*, or "no man may profit from his own wrong".

In other words, they argued that there was no use the company (at the behest of the liquidator) complaining that it should have been stopped from doing what it was dishonestly doing – any more than someone trying to break out of police custody should be able to sue the police for injuries sustained in the event (a not unknown phenomenon, as we have just seen).

In the High Court, the judge held that the company was primarily, not simply vicariously, responsible for the fraudulent conduct. S's fraud was properly attributed to the company. The judge further held that the *ex turpi causa* rule could not prevent a claim founded on fraud that would not have occurred had the auditors properly complied with their "very duty" as auditors of the company.

The Court of Appeal allowed the auditors' appeal. It ruled that since the company was a fraudster under the total control of another fraudster and was party to the fraud – and not itself a victim of the fraud – the auditors owed no duty of care to the company to take reasonable care to detect its fraud. Therefore, the claim against the auditors ought to be struck out. The company appealed to the House of Lords.

The law lords were divided three to two, which demonstrates the strength of the competing arguments. The decision of the majority proceeded thus: the company's controller, S, had been as bent as a nine bob note. The auditors should have stopped him. They did not. Ordinarily they would be liable in negligence. But they were being sued by the company. At law – and in fact – the company was the same as S: he was its sole shareholder and controlling mind. Therefore, the company was effectively saying that the auditors should have stopped it from committing fraud. That being so, if the company was to succeed in its claim, it would end up being compensated for its own wrongdoing.

The fact that the claim was being brought by the liquidators could make no difference, since it was an elementary principle of insolvency law that a liquidator could have no better claim against anyone than the company itself would have done.

Lord Brown – always one of the straightest talkers on the bench – used the following analogy: suppose a solicitor billed for 12 months' work over the course of a year, but fraudulently told his accountant about only six months' worth. The accountant should have spotted the omission but negligently failed to do so, and as a result only half of the fees was declared to the Revenue. The Revenue discovered the fraud and then required the solicitor to pay the balance together with penalties and costs. Could the solicitor then sue the accountant for not saving him from himself? Certainly not. Suppose too that the Revenue bankrupted the solicitor. Again, the fact that the solicitor would obtain a trustee in bankruptcy would make no difference: the trustee could have no better claim than the solicitor himself.

As there was no distinction between that hypothetical example and the present case the claim had to fail.

The *ratio* is accordingly that where the directing mind and will of the company is also its owner, and his fraudulent conduct is to be treated as the conduct of the company, *ex turpi causa* will defeat a claim by the company against the auditors.

As the judge at first instance had held, it would be artificial not to fix the company in the instant case with the knowledge and wrongdoing of S, and it would also be artificial to describe the company even as a secondary victim of the fraud.

All of the above sounds logical, even irresistibly so. But there were two problems. The first was that the reality was not that the case was being brought by what was left of the company, or the liquidators personally. The beneficiary of any recovery from the auditors would have been the company's creditors (in particular the bank which had sued S and the company in the first place and bankrupted it), and they were innocent victims of the auditors' (presumed) negligence. On the majority's holding, therefore, the auditors would gain an undeserved windfall in not being held to account for their negligence whilst the innocent bank would remain out of pocket.

The second problem was that the majority's holding was predicated on S being indivisible from the company, as its sole shareholder and controlling mind. Suppose, however, that there had been an innocent shareholder of just 1% of the company? S would still be the controlling mind but the 1% shareholder, not having done anything wrong, could not logically be stopped in his tracks by the *ex turpi causa* rule if he sued the auditors himself. Therefore, should the happenstance of a single share being held by an innocent party be a decisive factor? Or should it have to be 50% or more innocent shareholding or innocent board members? Or would the auditors only be liable for whatever percentage of the shareholding was innocent? None of those options seems satisfactory.

Yet another hypothetical example identifies the problem with the majority holding from the auditors' perspective. If they had done precisely the same negligent auditing, at precisely the same time, but in respect of a company where the controlling mind was innocent, they would have been liable without question. From their perspective the distinction would look distinctly odd.

The majority identified all of the above issues – then promptly ran a mile. They simply left it for another day.

Ordinarily it would be proper for a court not to deal with a question which did not fall for determination on the facts, unless it was a lower court and the point was threatened to be appealed. This case however involved a not atypical case of commercial fraud and had been fully argued before the House of Lords. In those circumstances it really behoved their lordships not to leave unanswered the serious questions about other hypothetical – but scarcely improbable – cases.

As it stands, in the light of their decision, the question of a similar case but involving innocent shareholding would be seriously arguable – all the way to the Supreme Court – with the resultant cost, delay and uncertainty to the litigants themselves and the commercial community generally whilst the final ruling was awaited. No one can be pleased with that.

Afterword: What Next for the Common Law?

The cases in this book have spanned over a century and a half, though in the context of the 1,000-year history of the common law that renders them all comparatively modern. I hope they have given some flavour of the legal system and how it has changed in the past few decades – and, equally, how it has not changed.

Far and away the greatest shocks to the legal system have occurred as a result of the two world wars, as I mentioned in the introduction to the Law and War section. Those conflicts and their aftermath gave us the rise of the regulatory state and then the equally strong influence of the European Union (EU) and the European Convention on Human Rights (the Convention). The EU began life as an attempt to link the heavy industry of France and Germany so as to ensure they could not go to war with each other again, while the Convention was an attempt to prevent any repeat of the repression of freedom leading up to the Second World War and the abominations that occurred during it.

I have not really touched on the EU as an institution in this book. I will therefore not attempt to debate the merits of its existence or its influence now, save to note

Much of this final piece is drawn from a blog in *Halsbury's Law Exchange*, published on 3 May 2012.

that one can be in favour of European union as a concept, but at the same time highly critical of the European Union as an actual institution. From the point of view of the common lawyer, even the greatest fans of the EU have to concede that it has introduced one important detriment – uncertainty – to the legal system.

To explain slightly further, in the past lawyers had to interpret domestic statutes. Apart from unravelling necessarily difficult wording, that often required tracing the legislative history of the enactment in question and any judicial treatment thereof. Nowadays the statute – or more likely a statutory instrument – might be passed in response to a European Directive. Thus the courts have to look at the wording of the Directive to see if there is any difference with that of the implementing instrument, then look to any relevant decisions by the European Court of Justice as well as domestic courts, and also apply what has been called the "strong interpretive techniques" of Brussels. In other words, they have to pay much less attention to the actual wording than they would normally do under a common law approach. Legal reasoning in many cases has never been quite the same since.

Note too that I have confined myself to a Sassenach perspective: north of the border my Scottish relatives have to contend with yet another layer of government and therefore arguments about the devolution settlement (and hence the *vires* of any decision said not to be within the Scottish Parliament's jurisdiction ...).

Rather more time in the book has been spent on the Convention and its supervising court in Strasbourg. The same objection as regards the EU – that it introduces a significant degree of uncertainty to the legal system – applies equally to the Convention. There is an old saying that everyone is in favour of fairness until someone tries to define it. Similarly, the rights and freedoms of the Convention are unobjectionable when stated as broad principles, but leave a wide scope for disagreement in any particular case. So wherever the Convention might be thought applicable, yet another factor is thrown in to the interpretive mix described above.

As if that were not enough, we also have a comparatively new beast in the form of the Charter of Fundamental Rights of the European Union, part of the price of the Lisbon treaty. It sets out fundamental rights that look rather similar to those of the Convention. It tells us:

> "In so far as this Charter contains rights which correspond to rights guaranteed by the Convention for the Protection of Human Rights and Fundamental Freedoms, the meaning and scope of those rights shall be the same as those laid down by the said Convention. This provision shall not prevent Union law providing more extensive protection."

Which may or may not be as clear as it sounds ...

It is true that the Convention was drafted by English lawyers and that it reflects the values of the common law as they had evolved over centuries. Moreover, for all the tabloid fodder, not all of Strasbourg's decisions (or domestic decisions made pursuant to the Convention) offend majority public opinion by any stretch of the imagination. In fact almost all applications brought there from Britain fail to get past the admissibility stage, and only a handful of those that do attract media interest (perhaps raising a separate issue about the advice and funding behind the multitude of failed applications).

It could also be argued that incurring some uncertainty in our domestic law and the odd derisory decision is a price worth paying for all of Europe – including former Communist countries with a shocking history of governance in the past century – to be subject to a regime of rights and freedoms based substantially on British values. The tale of Mr Uj the wine critic is but one example, and a mild one at that.

All that said, readers will have seen fundamental questions involving freedom of speech, freedom of religion, the right to life, the right to vote and so forth discussed in this book in the context of arguments before a court. Until the Human Rights Act 1998 brought the Convention into domestic law, most of those arguments would have been held before and settled by Parliament. In those days the true guarantee of freedom in Westminster countries was often said to be the regular ballot box, rather than some lawyers' document. It still remains questionable (i) whether the Convention and the Strasbourg court have sufficient democratic legitimacy, and (ii) whether the courts are a better forum to determine hotly contested ethical, moral and religious questions.

As to the first question, the democratic authorisation of the European Court comes from the fact that it was Parliament who passed the Human Rights Act 1998 and thereby brought the Convention within the jurisdiction of the domestic courts. Parliament always retains the option of withdrawing, though there would be turbulent international and domestic political fallout if it ever did so.

It should also be remembered that tyrannous regimes have sometimes come to power through elections. Further, the rights of the majority are rarely threatened: Convention rights, it can be argued, are needed to protect the unpopular minority.

Then again, we should be very careful about alternatives to majority rule. In the past we had to put up with monarchs asserting the divine right of kings. For centuries the churches bedevilled politics across Europe, and even in the present day there are bishops in the House of Lords *ex officio*. In other countries there have been military dictators or full-blown theocracies. It has been common for such undemocratic rulers to assure the people that they alone had special skills or knowledge or experience which the common people did not, and which therefore justified them overruling the common people's will as expressed through a legislature.

Human rights lawyers, therefore, are not the first to claim that they can and should be able to override parliament, and they are not in good company in that respect either, however benevolent their motives.

As to the second question, irrespective of whether one agrees with the answers they come up with, courts can only flesh out the broad detail of Convention rights slowly, as and when cases come before them, which leaves much uncertainty as well as handing significant power to the judges (government of the people by the judges for the lawyers went a saying when I was at law school). I should also add that the Strasbourg court is seriously in need of reform. It is severely overburdened, with many thousands of applications outstanding. It is composed of one judge from each member state – meaning that tiny political enclaves make the same contribution as countries with enormous legal resources such as Germany and Britain, which seems to me thoroughly illogical. The appointment process of some member states' judges is also questionable, as (probably consequentially) are the qualifications of some judges. I would repeat what I said with regard to prisoner voting: logic suggests that Strasbourg's supporters should also be the strongest advocates for its reform.

There were other possibilities for bringing British law into line with the Convention whenever it fell short. A cross-party committee primarily composed of legal experts could have studied Strasbourg decisions and advised whenever domestic law needed to be altered, for example. This would have answered any question about democratic legitimacy since any substantive change would have had to go through Parliament.

Still, I am not going to attempt to resolve the debate here. Whichever way one looks at it, we face a future in which the common law, for a mixture of good and bad reasons, will continue to be heavily influenced by Brussels and Strasbourg, and as a result will become even more complex than it already is. That means advice will be more expensive and more uncertain, and one does not need to be an economist or a soothsayer to understand the attendant disadvantages.

On the other hand, even in a country with the proud – indeed, unrivalled – history of individual liberty as Britain, there have been shameful abuses of state power and another layer of protection against tyranny should not lightly be dismissed. As the finishing touches were being put on this book, I read of someone being imprisoned in another country for writing something which to my eyes at least was an extraordinarily bland piece of theological naval gazing, but which the religious authorities in that country deemed a criminal offence. We need to be more grateful for our liberties in this country, and more protective of them as well.

Whatever happens with the legal system, one cannot envisage human nature fundamentally changing. That means that in one form or another, interesting philosophical questions, human dramas and logical puzzles will continue to appear in the law courts, as they always have, and, as this book has hopefully managed to show, always will.

James Wilson
July 2012

INDEX